Teatime
PARTIES

Teatime PARTIES

*Afternoon Tea to Commemorate
the Milestones of Life*

hm | books

hm | books

EDITOR *Lorna Reeves*
GROUP CREATIVE DIRECTOR *Deanna Rippy Gardner*
ART DIRECTOR *Leighann Lott Bryant*
ASSOCIATE EDITOR *Britt E. Stafford*
COPY EDITOR *Nancy Ogburn*
EDITORIAL ASSISTANT *Sarah Howard*
STYLIST *Lucy W. Herndon*
CREATIVE DIRECTOR/PHOTOGRAPHY
Mac Jamieson
SENIOR PHOTOGRAPHERS *John O'Hagan,*
Marcy Black Simpson
PHOTOGRAPHERS *Jim Bathie,*
William Dickey, Stephanie Welbourne
SENIOR DIGITAL IMAGING SPECIALIST
Delisa McDaniel
DIGITAL IMAGING SPECIALIST *Clark Densmore*
FOOD STYLIST/RECIPE DEVELOPER *Janet Lambert*
CONTRIBUTING FOOD STYLISTS/RECIPE DEVELOPERS
Susan D. Green, Virginia Hornbuckle, Kellie Gerber Kelley,
Elizabeth Stringer

hm
hoffmanmedia

CHAIRMAN OF THE BOARD/CEO
Phyllis Hoffman DePiano
PRESIDENT/COO *Eric W. Hoffman*
PRESIDENT/CCO *Brian Hart Hoffman*
EXECUTIVE VICE PRESIDENT/CFO *Mary P. Cummings*
**EXECUTIVE VICE PRESIDENT/OPERATIONS &
MANUFACTURING** *Greg Baugh*
VICE PRESIDENT/DIGITAL MEDIA *Jon Adamson*
VICE PRESIDENT/EDITORIAL *Cindy Smith Cooper*
**VICE PRESIDENT/INTEGRATED MARKETING
SOLUTIONS** *Ray Reed*
VICE PRESIDENT/ADMINISTRATION *Lynn Lee Terry*

Copyright © 2017 by Hoffman Media, LLC
Publishers of *TeaTime* magazine
teatimemagazine.com

Hoffman Media
1900 International Park Drive, Suite 50
Birmingham, Alabama 35243
hoffmanmedia.com

ISBN 978-1-940772-41-7
Printed in China

ON THE COVER: Sweets from Birthday, pages 100–102
ON THE BACK COVER: Bridal Shower, page 83

Goat Cheese, Lavender,
and Honey Mini Cheesecakes
PAGE 91

Contents

Introduction

WHAT BETTER WAY TO CELEBRATE LIFE'S SPECIAL EVENTS THAN WITH
AFTERNOON TEA? Milestones—such as birthdays, weddings, anniversaries, and
retirements—of people dear to us call for tea parties, with table settings and delectable
fare in keeping with the occasions. Whether casual or formal, modern or traditional,
serving four or 400, afternoon tea provides a memorable experience for all ages and
genders. After all, tea parties aren't just for little girls and elderly ladies.

In these pages, you will find beautifully set tables for 10 meaningful events that
touch virtually everyone's lives, each accompanied by menus and tea pairings to delight
your guests. Our "Tea-Steeping Guide" (page 125) provides expert recommendations
for preparing the perfect pot of tea to accompany the more than 90 recipes herein.
Whenever possible, we have included make-ahead tips for food preparation so you can
focus on other priorities the day of the party.

We understand that hosting a large gathering, especially for teatime, can be
somewhat daunting. In "Hosting Tea for a Crowd" (page 9), we provide helpful guidance
to make your event a success, including suggestions for serving buffet style.

Whatever the occasion that finds you gathering with family and friends, we offer
inspiration to make the milestone more meaningful by celebrating it with a tea party.

Hosting Tea FOR A CROWD

Many milestone celebrations, such as a graduation, a retirement, or a 50th wedding anniversary, might call for a guest list larger than that for a typical tea party. When faced with the task of preparing tea for a group, these helpful tips will ensure your event is a success whether you're a novice or an expert tea-party host.

EXTENDING INVITATIONS

Formal invitations are a lovely and thoughtful way to communicate the details of the upcoming event, as well as to be sure you have an accurate count of those who will attend. Although invitations printed or written by hand and mailed are certainly preferred, technology has made it acceptable to extend them via telephone or e-mail. However you choose to spread the word of your teatime celebration, plan early. Ideally, invitees should receive the communication a minimum of two weeks before the party. Invitations should include the following information:

- *Date and time of the event* (between 2:00 and 5:00 p.m., with 4:00 p.m. being preferred. If the format is a come-and-go reception, give a time range, such as 2:00 to 4:00 p.m.)

- *Address of venue*

- *Name of honoree(s)*

- *Name of host(s)*

- *Information and deadline for RSVP*

- *Preferred attire* (Specify only if clothing should be more formal or more casual than usual for afternoon tea or if costumes are encouraged.)

Roast Beef
Tea Sandwiches
PAGE 24

Blueberry
Scones with
Lemon Glaze
PAGE 43

PREPARING THE FOOD

Tea fare is usually best made *à la minute*, or just before serving. Unless you have a lot of help in the kitchen, it is often logistically impossible to wait until the day of the event to prepare the food. Many of the recipes in this book include a "MAKE-AHEAD TIP" section, but general tips for making favorite teatime fare in advance follow.

- *Scones*—Freeze raw scones on parchment-lined baking sheets. Once frozen, transfer scones to airtight containers or bags, and store in the freezer for up to a month. Just before serving, place desired quantity of frozen scones (do not thaw) on parchment-lined baking sheets, and bake in a preheated oven according to recipe, allowing an additional 5 to 10 minutes for adequate doneness and browning.

- *Tea Sandwiches*—Most fillings can be made a day ahead and stored in the refrigerator. Assemble sandwiches a few hours before the tea party, drape with damp paper towels, cover well with plastic wrap, and refrigerate until needed.

SELECTING AND SERVING HOT TEA

When choosing the types of tea to serve, offer a choice of at least two to accompany and complement your food selections. (The menus in this book feature a tea pairing for each of the courses.) Generally, strongly scented teas should be avoided. Instead, opt for classic blends, single-origin teas, or favorite fruit-flavored infusions. Having a caffeine-free alternative is a thoughtful gesture caffeine-sensitive guests will appreciate.

- *Use loose-leaf tea rather than prebagged. (See our "Tea-Steeping Guide" on page 125 for more information.)*

- *Make tea an hour or two ahead, and keep it hot in insulated urns or thermal carafes in the kitchen until ready to serve. (Do not use containers that have ever held coffee, as the lingering oils from the coffee will impart an unpleasant taste to the tea.)*

- *In the kitchen, warm teapots with hot water, discard water, and fill teapots with hot tea from urns or carafes just before serving.*

- *During the party, filled teapots can be placed on tea warmers (stands outfitted with tea lights) on the serving table or on individual tables, if desired. Because it is not possible to regulate the heat they produce, resulting in scorched tea, tea warmers are not suitable for keeping tea hot for long periods. (To prevent burns, please make sure children are closely supervised.) Tea cozies are a safe alternative to tea warmers and are available in many pretty and practical designs.*

- *Select several friends to ensure that pots and cups remain full throughout the event. Having others assist with this task allows you ample time to give guests your full attention while remaining a dutiful host, especially during a buffet-style tea party. So your pourers can still enjoy the tea party, write down a set schedule in which each person serves for no longer than 20 minutes.*

SETTING UP A BUFFET-STYLE TEA

The way you set up the food and tea can help avoid congestion when serving buffet style, such as our Retirement Tea on page 103. If possible, arrange the plates, napkins, pastry forks, small knives, and food on one table, and place the teapots, cups and saucers, teaspoons, and any condiments for the hot tea (milk, sugar and/or honey, and lemon slices) on a sideboard or a wet bar. If beverages and food will be served from the same table, group the tea things on the right end of the surface so guests can serve themselves tea fare first and pick up the hot tea last. Fare for a buffet-style event should consist mostly of finger foods to avoid the awkwardness of trying to balance a cup, plate, and silverware, especially if guests will be standing while partaking. Appropriate options can include tea sandwiches in assorted shapes, scones, small cupcakes, pastries, and cookies.

- *Snack plates—dishes with allotted space for a teacup—are a good alternative to traditional plates, cups, and saucers.*

- *When preparing food, planning for 2 or 3 of each item per guest can help prevent empty platters early into the event.*

- *Clearly designate a small table or other surface for used dishes.*

Baby
GENDER REVEAL

The
MENU

SCONE
Meyer Lemon Scones
Paris Garden Signature Tea

SAVORIES
Ham and Caramelized
Tomato Crostini

Lemony Roasted Asparagus
Pesto and Prawn Canapés

Roast Beef Tea Sandwiches
Ceylon Tea

SWEETS
Classic Shortbread
Sandwich Cookies

Cream Puffs

Browned Butter–Vanilla
Cupcakes

*Cherries & Cream Rooibos (girl)
or Açai Blueberry Signature Tea (boy)*

*Tea Pairings by Paris In A Cup,
714-538-9411, parisinacup.com*

*While they will certainly
enjoy the first two courses,
guests will anxiously
anticipate biting into
the centers of the sweets,
which contain the secret
of the baby's gender.*

Meyer Lemon Scones
Yield: 12

2 cups all-purpose flour
½ cup granulated sugar
2 teaspoons baking powder
¼ teaspoon salt
6 tablespoons cold unsalted butter, cut into pieces
2 tablespoons fresh Meyer lemon zest*
½ cup cold heavy whipping cream
1 large egg
1 teaspoon vanilla extract

• Preheat oven to 400°.
• Line a rimmed baking sheet with parchment paper.
• In a large bowl, combine flour, sugar, baking powder, and salt, whisking well. Using a pastry blender, cut butter into flour mixture until it resembles coarse crumbs. Add lemon zest, stirring until incorporated.
• In a medium bowl, combine cream, egg, and

vanilla extract, whisking until smooth. Gradually add cream mixture to flour mixture, stirring until mixture is evenly moist. (If dough seems dry, add more cream, 1 tablespoon at a time). Working gently, bring mixture together with hands until a dough forms.
• Turn out dough onto a lightly floured surface. Knead gently 4 to 5 times. Using a rolling pin, roll dough to a ½-inch thickness. Using a 2-inch fluted round cutter, cut 12 scones from dough, rerolling scraps as necessary. Refrigerate scones for 20 minutes.
• Bake until edges of scones are golden brown, 13 to 16 minutes.

One medium Meyer lemon yields approximately 1 tablespoon zest. Although Meyer lemons are sweeter than regular lemons, regular lemons can be substituted if Meyer lemons are not available.

RECOMMENDED CONDIMENT:
Meyer Lemon Whipped Cream (recipe follows)

Meyer Lemon Whipped Cream
Gluten-free | *Yield: 1¼ cups*

½ cup heavy whipping cream
1 tablespoon granulated sugar
¼ teaspoon vanilla extract
1 tablespoon fresh Meyer lemon zest
1 tablespoon fresh Meyer lemon juice*

• In a medium mixing bowl, combine cream, sugar, vanilla extract, lemon zest, and lemon juice. Beat at medium-high speed with a mixer fitted with the whisk attachment until soft peaks form.
• Serve immediately.

One medium Meyer lemon yields approximately 1 tablespoon zest. Although Meyer lemons are sweeter than regular lemons, regular lemons can be substituted if Meyer lemons are not available.

Ham and Caramelized Tomato Crostini
Yield: 12

1 loaf baguette bread
¾ cup extra-virgin olive oil
1 teaspoon sea salt, divided
½ teaspoon ground black pepper, divided
3 cloves garlic, peeled
3 large tomatoes, peeled and finely chopped
4 ounces shaved Serrano ham
2 ounces Manchego cheese

• Preheat oven to 400°.
• Line 2 rimmed baking sheets with parchment paper.
• Using a serrated bread knife, cut 12 (½-inch) diagonal slices from baguette. Lightly brush olive oil onto both sides of baguette slices. Sprinkle ½ teaspoon salt and ¼ teaspoon pepper evenly on one side of each slice. Place slices on prepared baking sheets. Toast until golden brown and lightly crisp, approximately 6 minutes.
• Immediately rub 2 garlic cloves on seasoned side of toasted baguette slices.
• In a large sauté pan, heat olive oil over medium-low heat. Add tomatoes, remaining 1 clove garlic, remaining ½ teaspoon salt, and remaining ¼ teaspoon pepper. Cook over medium-low heat, stirring occasionally, until tomatoes have thickened and darkened, 15 to 20 minutes. Remove garlic clove, and let tomatoes cool completely.
• Spread a thin layer of caramelized tomatoes onto seasoned side of toasted baguette slices. Top each slice with shaved Serrano ham, shingling to fit.
• Using a vegetable peeler, shave cheese. Arrange cheese shavings atop ham layer.
• Serve immediately.

MAKE-AHEAD TIP: Tomatoes can be caramelized a day ahead, placed in a covered container, and refrigerated. Bring to room temperature before using.

"A baby is coming, cute as can be.
Come find out if we're having
a he or a she!" —ANONYMOUS

- Preheat oven to 400°.
- Line 2 rimmed baking sheets with parchment paper.
- In a large pot, bring water to a boil. Add shrimp, 2 tablespoons lemon juice, bay leaf, peppercorns, and ½ teaspoon salt. Remove from heat. Stir gently until shrimp just turn pink and curl. Drain shrimp, and transfer to a large bowl filled halfway with iced water. Once shrimp are completely chilled, drain shrimp and let dry.
- Using a 2-inch round cutter, cut 12 rounds from frozen bread slices. Place in resealable plastic bag to prevent drying out, and let thaw at room temperature. Place bread rounds in a single layer on a prepared baking sheet.
- Lightly toast in oven until golden brown, approximately 6 minutes, turning as necessary.
- Snap or cut and discard tough ends from asparagus. Using a sharp knife, cut asparagus into 2-inch-long pieces. Place asparagus pieces in a single layer on remaining prepared baking sheet. Drizzle ¼ cup olive oil over asparagus, and sprinkle with 1 tablespoon lemon zest, ¼ teaspoon salt, and ⅛ teaspoon cracked pepper. Roast in oven until tender, 8 to 10 minutes. Let cool slightly.
- In a small skillet, heat walnuts over medium-low heat until lightly toasted and fragrant. Remove from pan, and let cool.
- Reserve 12 asparagus tips for garnish. In the bowl of a food processor, combine remaining asparagus, cheese, walnuts, garlic, 2 tablespoons olive oil, remaining 1 tablespoon lemon zest, remaining 2 tablespoons lemon juice, remaining ¼ teaspoon salt, and remaining ⅛ teaspoon cracked pepper, processing until smooth and scraping down sides of bowl as necessary. Gradually add remaining 2 tablespoons olive oil as needed until pesto is a thick but spreadable consistency.
- Spread a ¼-inch-thick layer of pesto onto toasted brioche rounds. Top each round with shrimp.
- Garnish each with a reserved asparagus tip and a parsley leaf, if desired.

*Zest lemons before juicing.

MAKE-AHEAD TIP: Shrimp can be cooked, chilled, and dried a day ahead. Place in an airtight container, and refrigerate until needed. Bread rounds can be cut out a day ahead and stored in a resealable plastic bag until needed.

Lemony Roasted Asparagus Pesto and Prawn Canapés
Yield: 1¼ cups

6 cups water
12 jumbo shrimp peeled, deveined, and tails removed
4 tablespoons lemon juice*, divided
1 bay leaf
1 teaspoon whole black peppercorns
1 teaspoon sea salt, divided
12 slices brioche bread, frozen
½ pound asparagus spears
½ cup olive oil, divided
2 tablespoons lemon zest, divided
¼ teaspoon cracked black pepper, divided
¼ cup walnuts
1 clove garlic
½ cup Parmesan cheese, coarsely grated
Garnish: 12 leaves Italian flat-leaf parsley

Roast Beef Tea Sandwiches
Yield: 12

12 slices thin white sandwich bread, frozen
12 slices thin whole-wheat sandwich bread, frozen
8 ounces shallot and chive-flavored gournay cheese
   spread, such as Boursin, softened
1 tablespoon finely chopped fresh Italian flat-leaf
   parsley
2 tablespoons heavy whipping cream
8 ounces thinly sliced deli roast beef
1½ cups baby arugula
½ teaspoon sea salt
¼ teaspoon cracked black pepper

• Using a 3x2-inch rectangular cutter, cut 12 rectangles from frozen white bread slices and 12 rectangles from frozen wheat bread slices, discarding scraps. Cover shapes with a damp paper towel, or place in a resealable plastic bag, to let thaw and prevent drying out.
• In a medium bowl, combine cheese spread and parsley, stirring well. Add cream, stirring until well combined and smooth.
• Spread a layer of cheese mixture onto each bread rectangle. Top 6 white bread rectangles and 6 wheat bread rectangles, cheese side up, with roast beef, shingling and trimming to fit. Place argula on top of roast beef, and season with salt and pepper. Top each white bread stack with a remaining wheat bread rectangle, cheese side down. Top each wheat bread stack with a remaining white bread rectangle, cheese side down.
• Serve immediately.

MAKE-AHEAD TIP: Sandwiches can be assembled, covered with damp paper towels, placed in a covered container, and refrigerated for up to 1 hour before serving.

Classic Shortbread Sandwich Cookies
Yield: 20

1 cup unsalted butter, softened
1 cup confectioners' sugar
1½ teaspoons vanilla extract
2 cups all-purpose flour
½ teaspoon salt
1 recipe Sweet Cream Cheese Filling (recipe follows)
Pink (for a girl) or blue (for a boy) paste food coloring
Garnish: ½ cup white nonpareils

• In a large mixing bowl, combine butter and confectioners' sugar. Beat at high speed with a mixer until creamy, approximately 2½ minutes. Add vanilla extract, beating until incorporated.
• In a medium bowl, combine flour and salt, whisking well. Add flour mixture to butter mixture, beating at low speed until a dough forms. Divide dough in half.
• Place half of dough between 2 sheets of parchment paper or wax paper. Using a rolling pin, roll dough to a ¼-inch thickness. Transfer dough and parchment paper to a rimmed baking sheet, and freeze for 15 minutes. Repeat with remaining dough.
• Preheat oven to 350°.
• Line 2 rimmed baking sheets with parchment paper.
• Remove dough from freezer, and remove parchment paper from dough. Place dough on a lightly floured surface.
• Using a 1½-inch fluted round cutter, cut 40 rounds from dough.* Place rounds 1 inch apart on prepared baking sheets.
• Bake until edges are light golden brown, 12 to 15 minutes. Let cool on baking sheets for 2 minutes. Transfer cookies to a wire rack, and let cool completely.
• Place 1 cup Sweet Cream Cheese Filling in a piping

bag fitted with a small star tip (Wilton #21). Pipe frosting around perimeter of flat side of 20 cookies in a spiral toward centers, leaving a ¼-inch space in the center.
• In a small bowl, tint remaining ¾ cup filling with food coloring until desired shade is achieved. Transfer tinted filling to a piping bag fitted with a small star tip (Wilton #21). Pipe tinted filling to fill space in center of each cookie. Top each with a remaining cookie, flat side down.
• Garnish visible filling on edges of cookies with a sprinkle of nonpareils, if desired.
• Place in an airtight container with layers separated by wax paper, and refrigerate for 30 minutes and up to a day.

If a higher yield is desired, scraps can be rerolled, frozen, and cut out. However, texture may be impacted slightly.

MAKE-AHEAD TIP: *Cookies can be baked in advance, placed in an airtight container with layers separated by wax paper, and frozen for up to a week. Let come to room temperature before filling.*

Sweet Cream Cheese Filling
Gluten-free | Yield: 2 cups

1 (8-ounce) package cream cheese, softened
½ cup unsalted butter, softened
3 cups confectioners' sugar
1 tablespoon vanilla extract

• In a medium mixing bowl, combine cream cheese and butter. Beat at medium speed with a mixer until creamy. Add confectioners' sugar and vanilla, beating until fluffy.
• Use immediately, or transfer to an airtight container, and refrigerate until needed. (Before using filling, let soften slightly at room temperature; beat with a mixer for 1 minute.)

Cream Puffs
Yield: 24

¾ cup water
6 tablespoons unsalted butter, cut into pieces
2 teaspoons granulated sugar
½ teaspoon salt
¾ cup all-purpose flour
3 large eggs, at room temperature
1 recipe Vanilla Pastry Cream (recipe follows)
2½ tablespoons seedless raspberry (for a girl) or
   blueberry (for a boy) fruit spread*, such as Polaner
Garnish: confectioners' sugar

- Preheat oven to 400°.
- Line 2 rimmed baking sheets with parchment paper.
- In a medium saucepan, combine water, butter, sugar, and salt over medium heat until butter melts. Add flour, stirring until dough pulls away from sides of pan, 1 to 2 minutes. Remove from heat, and let stand for 2 minutes, stirring a few times to cool dough. Add eggs, one at a time, stirring until each egg is well incorporated. (The dough will be smooth and shiny.)
- Transfer dough to a pastry bag fitted with a large round tip (Wilton #1A or Ateco #806). Pipe dough onto prepared baking sheet 1 inch apart in 1½-inch mounds. Pat dough peaks down with a damp finger.
- Bake until golden brown, approximately 20 minutes.
- Transfer baking sheet to a wire rack. Using a skewer or the tip of a pointed knife, poke a small hole in the side of each cream puff to allow steam to escape. Let cool completely.
- In a small bowl, combine Vanilla Pastry Cream and fruit spread, whisking until blended. Transfer tinted pastry cream to a piping bag fitted with a small round tip (Wilton #12). Pipe pastry cream into each cream puff through side hole to the fill center, being careful to wipe off any excess.
- Garnish cream puffs with a dusting of confectioners' sugar.
- Serve immediately.

Before using, make sure there are no fruit pieces that might be too large to pass through the piping tip.

MAKE-AHEAD TIP: *Cream puffs can be made a week in advance, placed (unfilled) in a single layer in heavy-duty resealable plastic bags, and frozen. Thaw completely before filling and garnishing.*

Vanilla Pastry Cream
Gluten-free | *Yield: 1¾ cups*

4 large egg yolks
½ cup granulated sugar
2 cups whole milk
3 tablespoons cornstarch
½ teaspoon salt
1 tablespoon unsalted butter, softened
1½ teaspoons vanilla extract

- In a medium bowl, combine egg yolks and sugar, whisking until well blended.
- In a medium saucepan, heat milk over medium-high heat until very hot, but not boiling.
- Gradually add hot milk, ¼ cup at a time, to egg mixture, whisking constantly. Add cornstarch and salt, whisking until incorporated. Using a fine-mesh sieve,

strain mixture into saucepan. Cook over medium heat, whisking constantly until mixture thickens. Remove from heat.
- Add butter and vanilla extract, whisking well.
- Transfer pastry cream to a heatproof container. Place plastic wrap on the surface of pastry cream to prevent it from forming a skin while cooling.
- Refrigerate until very cold, 4 to 6 hours or overnight, before using.

Browned Butter–Vanilla Cupcakes
Yield: 12

½ cup unsalted butter, softened
1 cup granulated sugar
2 large eggs
1½ cups cake flour, such as Swans Down
1½ teaspoons baking powder
¼ teaspoon salt
¼ cup whole milk
¼ cup sour cream
1 teaspoon vanilla extract
1 recipe Browned Butter Frosting (recipe follows), divided
Pink (for a girl) or blue (for a boy) paste food coloring

• Preheat oven to 350°.
• Line a 12-well muffin pan with paper liners.
• In a large mixing bowl, combine butter and sugar. Beat at high speed with a mixer until light and fluffy, 3 to 5 minutes. Add eggs, one at a time, beating well after each addition.
• In a medium bowl, combine flour, baking powder, and salt, whisking well.
• In a small bowl, combine milk, sour cream, and vanilla extract, whisking to blend.

• Add flour mixture to butter mixture in thirds, alternately with milk mixture, beginning and ending with flour mixture.
• Using a levered 3-tablespoon scoop, divide batter among wells of prepared pan.
• Bake until cupcakes are lightly browned and a wooden pick inserted in the centers comes out clean, 20 to 24 minutes. Let cupcakes cool completely before removing from pan.
• Using an apple corer, cut out center of each cupcake, creating a cavity. Reserve cupcake cores.
• Tint ½ cup Browned Butter Frosting with food coloring until desired shade is achieved. Transfer tinted frosting to a piping bag fitted with a medium round tip (Wilton #12). Pipe tinted frosting into center of each cupcake, filling cavities ¾ full. Top remainder of each cavity with reserved cupcake cores, trimming to fit and conceal tinted frosting.
• Place remaining 3½ cups Browned Butter Frosting in a piping bag fitted with a medium round tip (Wilton #12). Pipe frosting onto cupcakes in a decorative swirl.
• Serve immediately, or place cupcakes in a single layer in an airtight container, and refrigerate until ready to serve, up to a day. Let come to room temperature before serving.

Browned Butter Frosting
Gluten-free | *Yield: 4 cups*

2 cups unsalted butter
5 cups confectioners' sugar
¼ teaspoon salt
¼ cup whole milk
1½ teaspoons vanilla extract

• In a medium saucepan, heat butter over medium heat until browned and fragrant. (Watch carefully to prevent burnt butter.)
• Transfer browned butter to a heatproof container, and let cool. Cover and refrigerate until solidified, 4 to 6 hours.
• Let browned butter come to room temperature before using, approximately 30 minutes.
• In a large mixing bowl, combine browned butter, confectioners' sugar, salt, milk, and vanilla extract. Beat at low speed with a mixer, gradually increasing to high speed, until light and fluffy.
• Use immediately, or transfer to an airtight container, and refrigerate until needed, up to a day. (Before using frosting, let soften slightly at room temperature; beat with a mixer for 1 minute.)

Christening

MENU
The

SCONE
Orange-Pecan Scones
Golden Treasure Black Tea

SAVORIES
Peachy Deviled Eggs

Chicken-Cranberry
Tea Sandwiches

Strawberry-Cucumber
Rollups

*Flowery Jasmine
Before The Rain*

SWEETS
Walnut Butter Cookies

Ginger-Lime Tartlets

Lavender–White Chocolate
Petits Fours

*Pouchong Oolong
Sweet Jade Dew*

*Tea Pairings by Grace Tea Company,
978-635-9500, gracetea.com*

*Welcome the newest
addition to your family
with an intimate setting
and teatime treats as
delicate as your God-
given bundle of joy.*

Orange-Pecan Scones
Yield: 12

2 cups self-rising soft-wheat flour, such as White Lily
3 tablespoons granulated sugar
1 teaspoon fresh orange zest
¼ teaspoon kosher salt
⅓ cup cold salted butter, cut into pieces
½ cup chopped pecans
¾ cup whole buttermilk
1 teaspoon vanilla extract

• Preheat oven to 400°.
• Line a rimmed baking sheet with parchment paper.
• In a large bowl, combine flour, sugar, orange zest, and salt, whisking well. Using a pastry blender, cut butter into flour mixture until it resembles coarse crumbs. Add pecans, stirring until combined.
• In a small bowl, combine buttermilk and vanilla extract, stirring well. Add to flour mixture, stirring until evenly moist. (If dough seems dry, add more buttermilk, 1 tablespoon at a time.) Working gently, bring mixture together with hands until a dough forms.
• Turn out dough onto a lightly floured surface. Knead gently 3 or 4 times. Using a rolling pin, roll dough to a 1-inch thickness. Using a 2-inch square cutter, cut 12 scones from dough, rerolling scraps as necessary. Place scones 2 inches apart on prepared baking sheet.
• Bake until edges of scones are golden brown and a wooden pick inserted in the centers comes out clean, approximately 15 minutes.

RECOMMENDED CONDIMENTS:
Clotted Cream
Orange Marmalade

Peachy Deviled Eggs
Gluten-free | *Yield: 24*

12 large hard-cooked eggs, shelled
¼ cup finely chopped deli ham
¼ cup mayonnaise
2 tablespoons peach preserves
2 teaspoons chopped green onion
2 teaspoons apple cider vinegar
1 teaspoon yellow mustard
¼ teaspoon kosher salt
¼ teaspoon ground black pepper
Garnish: thin peach slices

• Using a sharp knife, cut eggs in half lengthwise. Carefully remove yolks, and place in a medium bowl. Set aside egg white halves.
• Using a fork, finely mash yolks. Add ham, mayonnaise, peach preserves, green onion, apple cider vinegar, mustard, salt, and pepper, stirring until combined.
• Transfer yolk mixture to a piping bag fit with a medium open-star tip (Wilton #1M). Pipe mixture evenly into egg white halves.
• Garnish each with a peach slice, if desired.

Chicken-Cranberry Tea Sandwiches
Yield: 18

1½ cups finely chopped rotisserie chicken
½ cup finely chopped dried sweetened cranberries,
    such as Craisins
⅓ cup finely chopped celery
¼ cup chopped toasted almonds
2 tablespoons chopped fresh chives
½ cup mayonnaise
¼ cup sour cream
¼ teaspoon kosher salt
¼ teaspoon ground black pepper
12 slices thin whole-wheat bread
½ cup chopped arugula

• In a medium bowl, combine chicken, cranberries, celery, almonds, and chives, stirring well.
• In a small bowl, combine mayonnaise, sour cream, salt, and pepper, stirring well to blend. Add to chicken mixture, stirring to coat.
• Using a serrated bread knife, trim and discard crusts from bread slices.
• Spread an even layer of chicken mixture onto 6 bread slices. Top each with arugula and a remaining bread slice.
• Using a serrated bread knife, cut each sandwich into 3 fingers.
• Serve immediately.

MAKE-AHEAD TIP: Sandwiches can be assembled, covered with damp paper towels, placed in a covered container, and refrigerated for up to 1 hour before serving.

Strawberry-Cucumber Rollups
Gluten-free | *Yield: 24*

3 English cucumbers
1 (8-ounce) package cream cheese, softened
½ cup diced strawberries
⅓ cup mayonnaise
¼ cup minced red onion
2 tablespoons finely chopped fresh basil
¼ teaspoon kosher salt
¼ teaspoon ground black pepper
Garnish: small basil leaves

• Using a mandoline or a sharp knife, cut 24 (6-inch-long) thin cucumber slices. Place slices on several layers of paper towels. Let stand for 15 minutes.
• In a medium bowl, combine cream cheese, strawberries, mayonnaise, onion, chopped basil, salt, and pepper, stirring until blended.

• Spoon strawberry mixture onto one end of each cucumber slice. Roll up, encasing strawberry mixture, and secure with wooden picks.
• Garnish each rollup with a basil leaf, if desired.
• Serve immediately, or place in an airtight container and refrigerate for up to an hour.

- In a shallow dish, dredge cookies in remaining 1 cup confectioners' sugar.
- Serve immediately, or store at room temperature in an airtight container with layers separated by wax paper for up to a day.

Ginger-Lime Tartlets
Yield: 24

½ cup salted butter, softened
⅔ cup plus ½ cup granulated sugar, divided
1 large egg white
1¼ cups all-purpose flour
1 teaspoon ground ginger
2 large eggs
¼ cup plus 2 teaspoons fresh lime zest, divided
3 tablespoons fresh lime juice
2 tablespoons salted butter, melted
½ cup heavy whipping cream

- Preheat oven to 325°.
- Spray 2 (12-well) mini muffin pans with cooking spray.
- In a large mixing bowl, combine ½ cup butter and ⅓ cup sugar. Beat at high speed with a mixer until creamy. Add egg white, beating until incorporated. Add flour and ginger, beating until well blended.
- Divide dough evenly into 24 balls, and place a dough ball in each well of prepared pans. Using a well-floured tamper or fingers, press dough into bottoms and up sides of wells.
- In a medium bowl, whisk eggs until light in color. Add ⅓ cup sugar, 2 teaspoons lime zest, lime juice, and melted butter, stirring until sugar dissolves. Divide egg mixture among wells of prepared pans.
- Bake until lightly golden brown, approximately 20 minutes. Let cool in pans for 5 minutes. Transfer tartlets to a wire cooling rack, and let cool completely.
- In a small bowl, combine remaining ½ cup sugar and remaining ¼ cup lime zest, tossing to coat. Transfer mixture to a fine-mesh sieve, and shake to remove excess sugar from zest.
- Just before serving, in a medium mixing bowl, beat cream at high speed with a mixer until stiff peaks form. Spoon whipped cream evenly onto tartlets. Sprinkle tartlets with sugared lime zest.
- Serve immediately.

MAKE-AHEAD TIP: Tartlets can be made a day in advance, placed in a single layer in an airtight container, and refrigerated until needed. Top with whipped cream and sugared lime zest just before serving.

Walnut Butter Cookies
Yield: approximately 60

1 cup salted butter, softened
2 cups confectioners' sugar, divided
1¾ cups all-purpose flour
1 cup chopped walnuts
1 teaspoon vanilla extract

- In a large mixing bowl, combine butter and 1 cup confectioners' sugar. Beat at medium speed with a mixer until light and creamy. Add flour, walnuts, and vanilla extract, beating until blended.
- Divide dough in half and roll each half into an 8-inch log. Wrap logs in plastic wrap, and refrigerate overnight.
- Preheat oven to 350°.
- Line several rimmed baking sheets with parchment paper.
- Unwrap logs. Using a sharp knife, cut logs into ⅛-inch slices. Place slices 2 inches apart on prepared baking sheets. Freeze for 15 minutes.
- Bake until edges of cookies are golden brown, approximately 12 minutes. Remove from baking sheets, and let cool completely on wire racks.

- Preheat oven to 350°.
- Spray a 13x9-inch baking pan with baking spray. Line pan with parchment paper.
- In a medium bowl, combine flour, baking powder, and salt, whisking well.
- In a large mixing bowl, combine butter and sugar. Beat at high speed with a mixer until creamy. Add eggs, one at a time, beating well after each addition. Add sour cream and extracts, beating until well blended. Add flour mixture to butter mixture, beating at low speed just until blended. Spread batter into prepared pan, smoothing top to make a flat surface.
- Bake until a wooden pick inserted in the center comes out clean, approximately 25 minutes. Let cool completely in pan. Wrap cake in pan well with plastic wrap, and let sit at room temperature for 6 to 8 hours.
- Unwrap cake and turn out onto a cutting board. Remove parchment paper.
- Using a 1½-inch square cutter, cut 34 squares from cake, avoiding sides of cake. Place cake squares on a wire cooling rack set over a rimmed baking sheet.
- Pour White Chocolate Icing over cake squares, covering completely and using a small offset spatula, if needed, to spread icing. (If necessary, excess icing that pools on rimmed baking sheet can be scraped off, reheated, and re-used.)
- Refrigerate cake squares on wire rack until icing sets, approximately 2 hours. Once icing sets, transfer cake squares to an airtight container, and refrigerate until ready to serve.
- Just before serving, garnish with melted white chocolate, white chocolate curls, or fresh or dried lavender, if desired.

Lavender–White Chocolate Petits Fours
Yield: 34

1¾ cups all-purpose flour
½ teaspoon baking powder
½ teaspoon kosher salt
1 cup salted butter, softened
1 cup granulated sugar
4 large eggs
¼ cup sour cream
½ teaspoon vanilla extract
½ teaspoon lavender extract
1 recipe White Chocolate Icing (recipe follows)
Garnish: melted white chocolate, white chocolate
   curls, or fresh or dried culinary lavender

White Chocolate Icing
Gluten-free | *Yield: approximately 3 cups*

6 cups confectioners' sugar
½ cup water
2 tablespoons light corn syrup
¼ teaspoon vanilla extract
¾ cup white chocolate morsels

- In the top of a double boiler, combine confectioners' sugar, water, corn syrup, and vanilla extract, whisking until well blended. Place over simmering water, and cook until temperature reaches 90° on a candy thermometer. Add chocolate morsels, stirring until melted and smooth.
- Keep warm over steaming water. Use immediately.

First
TEA PARTY

The
MENU

SCONE

Blueberry Scones
with Lemon Glaze

Dragonfruit Rooibos

SAVORIES

Creamy PBJ
Triple Stacks

Egg Salad
in Puff Pastry Baskets

Turkey and American
Grilled Cheese

Snickerdoodle Rooibos

SWEETS

Mini Vanilla Rosette
Cupcakes

Lemon Zest
Linzer Cookies

Mini Strawberry
Bundt Marshmallows

*Beatrix Potter's
Herbal Tisane Blend*

*Tea Pairings by Simpson & Vail, Inc.,
800-282-8327, svtea.com*

*Children will adore the
simple, playful, and
refined styles of their
first tea party with fare
even the pickiest eater
won't refuse.*

"I said so politely
While lifting my cup,
'The child in my heart
should never grow up.'"

—SALLY BOYD LONG

- Preheat oven to 350°.
- Line a rimmed baking sheet with parchment paper.
- In a large bowl, combine flour, sugar, baking powder, lemon zest, and salt, whisking well. Using a pastry blender, cut butter into flour mixture until it resembles coarse crumbs. Add dried blueberries, stirring until incorporated.
- In a liquid-measuring cup, combine ¾ cup cream and vanilla extract, whisking well. Add to flour mixture, stirring until mixture is evenly moist. (If dough seems dry, add more cream, 1 tablespoon at a time.) Working gently, bring mixture together with hands until a dough forms.
- Turn out dough onto a lightly floured surface. Knead gently 4 to 5 times. Using a rolling pin, roll dough to a ¾-inch thickness. Using a 2½-inch heart-shaped cutter, cut 10 scones from dough, rerolling scraps as necessary. Place scones 2 inches apart on prepared baking sheet.
- Brush tops of scones with remaining 1 tablespoon cream.
- Bake until edges of scones are golden brown and a wooden pick inserted in the centers comes out clean, approximately 18 minutes.
- Using a spoon, drizzle Lemon Glaze on warm scones.
- Serve immediately.

RECOMMENDED CONDIMENT:
Clotted Cream

Blueberry Scones with Lemon Glaze
Yield: 10

2 cups all-purpose flour
⅓ cup granulated sugar
2 teaspoons baking powder
1 teaspoon fresh lemon zest
½ teaspoon salt
4 tablespoons cold salted butter, cut into pieces
½ cup chopped dried blueberries
¾ cup plus 1 tablespoon cold heavy whipping cream, divided
½ teaspoon vanilla extract
1 recipe Lemon Glaze (recipe follows)

Lemon Glaze
Gluten-free | *Yield: ½ cup*

½ cup confectioners' sugar
½ teaspoon fresh lemon zest
1½ tablespoons heavy whipping cream
½ tablespoon fresh lemon juice

- In a liquid-measuring cup, combine confectioners' sugar, lemon zest, cream, and lemon juice, stirring to combine.
- Use immediately.

Creamy PBJ Triple Stacks

Yield: 6

18 slices very thin white bread, frozen
½ cup cream cheese, softened
½ cup confectioners' sugar
1 cup creamy peanut butter
¾ cup grape jelly

• Using a 3-inch flower-shaped cutter, cut 18 shapes
from frozen bread slices, discarding scraps. Set 12
bread shapes aside. Using a 1½-inch flower-shaped
cutter, cut a shape from centers of remaining 6 bread
shapes, discarding centers. Cover all bread shapes
with damp paper towels, or store in a reasealable
plastic bag to thaw and prevent drying out.
• In a small bowl, combine cream cheese and confectioners' sugar, stirring until smooth. Transfer cream
cheese mixture to a piping bag fitted with a small star
tip (Wilton #18).
• Spread an even layer of peanut butter onto each
of 6 solid bread shapes. Pipe a layer of cream cheese
mixture on top of peanut butter layer, following the
contours of the bread shapes. Top each with a solid
bread shape. Spread an even layer of grape jelly onto
each stack. Top each with a flower shape with cutout.
• Cover with damp paper towels, and let bread thaw
completely (approximately 30 minutes) before serving.

Egg Salad in Puff Pastry Baskets

Yield: 12

4 hard-cooked eggs, peeled
¼ teaspoon salt
3 tablespoons mayonnaise
1½ tablespoons sour cream
1½ tablespoons Dijon-style mustard
1½ tablespoons sweet pickle relish
1 (9.5-ounce) package frozen puff pastry cups,
   slightly thawed
Garnish: minced fresh chives

• In the bowl of a food processor, combine eggs, salt,
mayonnaise, sour cream, mustard, and pickle relish,
pulsing until smooth. Cover, and refrigerate until cold,
approximately 4 hours.
• Preheat oven to 400°.
• Line a rimmed baking sheet with parchment paper.
• Place puff pastry cups 2 inches apart on prepared
baking sheet.
• Bake until golden brown, 10 to 15 minutes. Press
center of cups down to create a cavity for the filling.
Let cool completely.

• Transfer egg mixture to a piping bag fitted with a
medium open-star tip (Wilton #32). Pipe a decorative
swirl into each puff pastry cup.
• Garnish with chives, if desired.
• Serve immediately, or refrigerate, lightly covered, for
up to 30 minutes before serving.

Turkey and American Grilled Cheese

Yield: 6

6 slices sourdough bread, frozen
3 slices deli turkey
3 slices white American cheese
3 tablespoons Dijon-style mustard
3 tablespoons mayonnaise
1 tablespoon butter

• Using a 3-inch square cutter, cut 6 squares from
frozen bread slices, discarding scraps.
• Using the same square cutter, cut 3 squares from
turkey slices and 3 squares from cheese slices, discarding scraps.
• Spread 1 tablespoon mustard onto each of 3 bread
squares. Top each with a cheese square and a turkey
square. Spread 1 tablespoon mayonnaise onto each
of remaining 3 bread squares. Place on top of turkey
layer, mayonnaise side down.
• Preheat a nonstick sauté pan over medium heat.
Melt butter in pan. Add sandwiches to pan, and toast
on both sides until golden brown and cheese begins
to melt, approximately 1 minute per side. Remove
from pan, and let cool slightly.
• Using a large sharp knife in a downward motion, cut
sandwiches in half diagonally to create 2 triangles.
• Serve immediately.

Mini Vanilla Rosette Cupcakes
Yield: 38

½ cup salted butter, softened
1 cup granulated sugar
2 large eggs
1½ cups all-purpose flour
½ teaspoon baking powder
¼ teaspoon salt
⅔ cup whole milk
½ teaspoon vanilla extract
½ teaspoon almond extract
1 recipe Vanilla Buttercream (recipe follows)

• Preheat oven to 350°.
• Line 38 wells of a 48-well mini muffin pan with paper liners.
• In a large mixing bowl, combine butter and sugar. Beat at high speed with a mixer until light and fluffy, 3 to 5 minutes. Add eggs, one at a time, beating well after each addition.
• In a medium bowl, combine flour, baking powder, and salt, whisking well.
• In a liquid-measuring cup, combine milk and extracts. Add flour mixture to butter mixture in thirds, alternately with milk mixture, beginning and ending with flour mixture.
• Using a levered 2-teaspoon scoop, divide batter among prepared wells of muffin pan.
• Bake until a wooden pick inserted in the centers comes out clean, 11 to 12 minutes. Let cupcakes cool completely in the pan on a wire cooling rack.
• Place Vanilla Buttercream in a piping bag fitted with a small closed-star tip (Wilton #30), and pipe a rosette on top of cupcakes.
• Serve immediately, or place cupcakes in a single layer in an airtight container, and refrigerate until ready to serve, up to a day.

KITCHEN TIP: For buttercream rosette, hold bag upright, and starting in the center, pipe frosting in a spiral.

Vanilla Buttercream
Gluten-free | *Yield: 1½ cups*

¾ cup salted butter, softened
2½ cups confectioners' sugar
1 tablespoon milk
3 drops neon purple food coloring
3 drops royal purple food coloring

• In a large mixing bowl, beat butter at high speed with a mixer until creamy. Add confectioners' sugar, milk, and food coloring, beating at low speed. Gradually increase to high speed, beating until light and fluffy.
• Use immediately.

Lemon Zest Linzer Cookies
Yield: 24

3¼ cups all-purpose flour
½ teaspoon salt
¼ teaspoon baking powder
1 cup salted butter, softened
1¼ cups granulated sugar
2 large eggs
½ tablespoon fresh lemon zest
¾ cup prepared lemon curd

• Preheat oven to 350°.
• Line several rimmed baking sheets with parchment paper.
• In a medium bowl, combine flour, salt, and baking powder, whisking well.
• In a large mixing bowl, combine butter and sugar. Beat at high speed with a mixer until light and fluffy, approximately 5 minutes. Add eggs and lemon zest, beating until incorporated. Gradually add flour mixture to butter mixture, beating until dough comes together. Divide dough in half.
• Place half of dough between 2 sheets of parchment paper or wax paper. Using a rolling pin, roll dough to a ¼-inch thickness. Transfer dough and parchment paper to a rimmed baking sheet, and freeze for 15 minutes. Repeat with remaining dough.
• Remove dough from freezer, and remove parchment paper from dough. Place dough on a lightly floured surface.
• Using a 2-inch fluted round cutter fitted with a teacup- or teapot-shaped linzer cutter*, cut 12 rounds from chilled dough, and remove and discard centers. Remove linzer cutter, and cut 12 whole rounds from remaining dough. Place all rounds 2 inches apart on prepared baking sheets.
• Bake until edges of cookies are the palest golden

brown, approximately 8 minutes. Transfer cookies to wire racks, and let cool completely.
• Store at room temperature in an airtight container with layers separated by wax paper until ready to serve.
• Just before serving, spread a thin layer of lemon curd onto each whole cookie. Top with a cut-out cookie. If needed, fill linzer shape with more lemon curd.

We used a Linzer Tea & Coffee Cookie Cutter Set available at Fancy Flours, 406-587-0118, fancyflours.com.

Mini Strawberry Bundt Marshmallows
Gluten-free | Yield: 24

3 tablespoons unflavored gelatin powder
½ cup cold water
1¾ cups granulated sugar
⅛ teaspoon salt
⅓ cup plus 1 tablespoon tap water
¾ cup light corn syrup
2 teaspoons strawberry extract
Pink paste food coloring, such as Wilton
Lavender sugar sprinkles
Confectioners' sugar (for dusting)

• In a small microwave-safe bowl, combine gelatin powder and cold water, stirring until blended.
• In a medium saucepan, combine granulated sugar, salt, and tap water. Bring to a boil until temperature reaches 240° on a candy thermometer, approximately 10 minutes.
• Heat gelatin in the microwave until liquefied, approximately 15 seconds.
• Transfer gelatin to a medium heat-proof mixing bowl. Add corn syrup, beating at low speed with a mixer fitted with a whisk attachment. Gradually add hot sugar syrup to gelatin mixture. Increase to medium speed, whisking until fluffy, 8 to 9 minutes. Add strawberry extract and food coloring until desired color is achieved, whisking until combined.
• Transfer mixture to a piping bag fitted with a small circular tip (Wilton #10).
• Spray 24 wells of mini Bundt molds* with cooking spray. Sprinkle lavender sprinkles into each prepared well. Pipe marshmallow mixture into each well. Dust with confectioners' sugar. Leave to dry at room temperature for at least 5 hours.
• Invert each cavity to release marshmallows.
• Toss marshmallows in more confectioners' sugar, if desired. Using a pastry brush, brush off excess.

We used 15-well (1⅝-inch) Mini Bundt Silicone Cake Molds available at Hobby Lobby, hobbylobby.com.

The
MENU

SCONE
Funfetti Scones
Organic Strawberry Oolong

SAVORIES
Veggie Pizza Swirls
BLT Stacks with Avocado
Teriyaki Turkey Sliders
Fountain of Youth Açai

SWEETS
Pink Raspberry
French Macarons

Mini Strawberry
Flower Tartlets

Chocolate Cake with
White Chocolate
Buttercream Frosting
Lemon Drop

Tea Pairings by Capital Teas,
888-484-8327, capitalteas.com

*Transform a typical
birthday party into a
sophisticated yet fun
celebration with a menu
that incorporates pops
of color and a variety of
fabulous flavors.*

Funfetti Scones
Yield: 12

2½ cups all-purpose flour
⅓ cup granulated sugar
2¼ teaspoons baking powder
½ teaspoon salt
6 tablespoons cold unsalted butter, cut into pieces
¼ cup bright rainbow sprinkles*
¾ cup plus 2 tablespoons cold heavy whipping
    cream, divided
1 large egg
½ teaspoon vanilla extract
¼ teaspoon almond extract

• Preheat oven to 350°.
• Line a rimmed baking sheet with parchment paper.
• In a large bowl, combine flour, sugar, baking powder, and salt, whisking well. Using a pastry blender, cut butter into flour mixture until it resembles coarse crumbs. Add sprinkles, stirring until incorporated.
• In a medium bowl, combine ¾ cup plus 1 tablespoon cream, egg, vanilla extract, and almond extract, whisking well. Add to flour mixture, stirring until mixture is evenly moist. (If dough seems dry, add more cream, 1 tablespoon at a time.) Working gently, bring mixture together with hands until a dough forms.
• Turn out dough onto a lightly floured surface. Knead gently 4 to 5 times. Using a rolling pin, roll dough to a ¾-inch thickness. Using a 2¼-inch round cutter, cut 12 scones from dough, rerolling scraps as necessary. Place scones 2 inches apart on prepared baking sheet.
• Brush tops of scones with remaining 1 tablespoon cream.
• Bake until edges are golden brown and a wooden pick inserted in centers comes out clean, approximately 20 minutes.
• Serve warm.

*We used Sunny Side Up Bakery Rainbow Sprinkles, available at Hobby Lobby, hobbylobby.com.

RECOMMENDED CONDIMENTS:
Clotted Cream
Strawberry Jam

"May you always have walls for the winds, a roof for the rain, tea beside the fire, laughter to cheer you, those you love near you, and all your heart may desire." —IRISH BLESSING

Veggie Pizza Swirls
Yield: 24

2 tablespoons olive oil
1 cup chopped green bell pepper
1 cup chopped white button mushrooms
1 (17.3-ounce) package frozen puff pastry (2 sheets)
⅓ cup prepared pizza sauce
1 cup shredded mozzarella cheese
1 (4-ounce) package goat cheese
¼ cup finely chopped black olives
1 large egg
1 tablespoon water

• In a medium sauté pan, heat olive oil over medium-high heat. Add bell pepper and mushrooms, stirring well. Reduce heat to medium-low, and cook, stirring occasionally, until tender, 3 to 5 minutes. Let cool.
• Let puff pastry thaw just enough to be able to roll up and encase filling. (It should still be cold and firm.)
• On a lightly floured surface, unfold both puff pastry sheets. Using a rolling pin, roll out puff pastry to a ⅛-inch thickness. Spread pizza sauce evenly onto puff pastry sheets, leaving a 1-inch margin around edges. Sprinkle mozzarella cheese evenly over sauce. Pinch pieces from goat cheese, and sprinkle over mozzarella layer. Scatter cooked vegetables and olives over cheeses.
• Starting at a long end, roll up each pastry firmly and evenly to encase ingredients and form a cylinder. Tuck ends under. Wrap each cylinder securely in plastic wrap, and refrigerate until cold, approximately 4 hours and up to a day.
• Preheat oven to 400°.
• Line 2 rimmed baking sheets with parchment paper.
• Remove cylinders from plastic wrap. Using a serrated knife in a sawing motion, cut 12 slices from each. Place slices 2 inches apart on prepared baking sheets.
• In a small bowl, combine egg and water, whisking well to blend. Brush slices with egg mixture.
• Bake until golden brown, 13 to 15 minutes.
• Serve warm.

Teriyaki Turkey Sliders

Yield: 9

2 tablespoons plus ½ teaspoon olive oil
9 canned pineapple slices, well drained
1 tablespoon unsalted butter
½ cup chopped sweet onion
½ cup chopped red bell pepper
1 (1.3-pound) package ground turkey breast meat
2 teaspoons finely grated fresh ginger
½ teaspoon salt
¼ teaspoon ground black pepper
1 large egg white
4 tablespoons teriyaki sauce, divided
½ cup mayonnaise
3 tablespoons finely chopped fresh basil
9 slider buns
9 leaves green leaf lettuce

• Preheat oven to 350°.
• Line a rimmed baking sheet with foil.
• Heat a large nonstick sauté pan, lightly brushed with ½ teaspoon olive oil, over high heat. Sear both sides of pineapple slices until lightly caramelized. Remove pineapple slices to a plate.
• In the same large sauté pan, melt butter over medium-high heat. Add onion and bell pepper. Reduce heat to medium-low, and cook, stirring occasionally, until tender, 3 to 5 minutes. Let cool.
• In a large bowl, combine ground turkey, cooled vegetables, ginger, salt, pepper, egg white, and 2 tablespoons teriyaki sauce, stirring well. Using a ¼-cup levered scoop, divide mixture into 9 even portions. Shape portions into patties.
• In a large nonstick sauté pan, heat remaining 2 tablespoons olive oil over medium-high heat until oil shimmers. Add patties to pan, and cook until nicely browned, approximately 2 minutes per side. Add remaining 2 tablespoons teriyaki sauce to pan, and turn patties to coat with sauce. (Patties should be pink inside.) Place patties 2 inches apart on prepared baking sheet.
• Bake patties until juices run clear when pressed or until a meat thermometer registers 170°, approximately 10 minutes.
• In a small bowl, combine mayonnaise and basil, stirring well. Spread basil mayonnaise onto cut surfaces of buns. Place a lettuce leaf on bottom half of each bun, and top each with a pineapple slice, a turkey patty, and top half of bun, mayonnaise side down.
• Serve immediately.

MAKE-AHEAD TIP: Turkey patties can be prepared up to a day ahead, placed in an airtight container, and refrigerated. Cook just before serving.

BLT Stacks with Avocado

Yield: 12

18 slices very thin white bread, frozen
¼ cup mayonnaise
½ cup baby spinach leaves
12 (3¾-inch-long) slices cooked bacon
12 slices Campari tomato
12 (3¾-inch-long) slices avocado

• Using a 2¾-inch square cutter, cut 18 shapes from frozen bread, discarding scraps. Using a sharp knife in a downward motion, cut each square in half diagonally. Let bread thaw.
• Heat a large nonstick sauté pan over medium-high heat. Toast bread slices in pan, turning to toast both sides. Let cool slightly.
• Spread an even layer of mayonnaise onto each bread triangle. Place a spinach leaf on mayonnaise side of each of 12 bread triangles. Top each with a bacon slice and a bread triangle, mayonnaise side up. Top each with a tomato slice, an avocado slice, and a remaining bread triangle, mayonnaise side down.
• Secure with decorative pick, if desired.
• Serve immediately.

Pink Raspberry French Macarons
Gluten-free | *Yield: 36*

2½ cups confectioners' sugar
2½ cups almond flour, such as Bob's Red Mill
6 large egg whites, at room temperature, divided
Pink food coloring paste, such as Wilton
1 cup granulated sugar
¼ cup water
⅛ teaspoon egg white powder
1 teaspoon raspberry extract
1 (8-ounce container) mascarpone cheese
⅓ cup seedless raspberry jam

• In the work bowl of a food processor, combine confectioners' sugar and almond flour, pulsing just to combine.
• In a large mixing bowl, combine 3 egg whites and almond flour mixture. Beat at medium speed with a mixer until light and fluffy. Add desired amount of food coloring to tint almond mixture.
• In a small saucepan, heat granulated sugar and water over medium heat. Cook until mixture reaches soft-ball stage (234° to 240° on a candy thermometer).
• In the bowl of a stand mixer fitted with whisk attachment, beat remaining 3 egg whites at high speed until soft peaks form. Slowly add hot syrup to egg whites, beating at medium-high speed until meringue has thickened and cooled, 3 to 5 minutes. (Bowl should be slightly warm to the touch.) Add egg white powder and raspberry extract, beating until incorporated. Using a rubber spatula, gradually fold meringue into almond mixture, a little at a time, until combined and batter is loose. (Batter should fall in thick ribbons from the spatula.)
• Preheat oven to 270°.
• Line several rimmed baking sheets with a silicone baking mat or parchment paper.
• Transfer batter to a piping bag fitted with a medium round tip (Wilton #12). Pipe batter onto prepared pans in silver dollar–size rounds. Drop pans onto countertops several times to release air bubbles.
• Let stand for 20 minutes to create a skin on macarons. (Macarons should feel dry to the touch and should not stick to the finger.)
• Bake until firm to the touch, 17 to 20 minutes.
• Let cool completely on pans. Gently wrap macarons in groups of 6 in plastic wrap, and place in an airtight container. Refrigerate overnight before filling.
• Place mascarpone cheese in a piping bag fitted with a medium round tip (Wilton #12), and pipe a circle around edge of flat side of half of macarons. Place ¼ teaspoon raspberry jam inside mascarpone circles. Top with remaining macarons, flat sides down.
• Keep refrigerated until ready to serve, up to a day.

Mini Strawberry Flower Tartlets

(Pictured opposite and on page 133.)
Yield: 12

4 ounces cream cheese, softened
2 tablespoons confectioners' sugar
½ tablespoon heavy whipping cream
⅛ teaspoon vanilla extract
12 large strawberries
1 kiwi
12 (1.75-inch) mini shortbread tartlet shells,
   such as Clearbrook Farms

• In a small mixing bowl, combine cream cheese, confectioners' sugar, whipping cream, and vanilla extract. Beat at medium-high speed with a mixer until smooth.
• Transfer mixture to a piping bag fitted with a medium round tip (Wilton #12). Pipe mixture into tartlet shells, creating a level surface.
• Using a sharp paring knife, cut each strawberry into ⅛-inch-thick horizontal slices.
• Using a sharp paring knife, peel kiwi, and cut into 6 (⅛-inch-thick) horizontal slices. Cut each kiwi slice in half, then into 3 wedges per half.
• Arrange strawberry slices in cream in tartlet shells to resemble flowers, overlapping as needed until tartlets are filled.
• Insert 3 kiwi wedges each between strawberry flowers and tartlet shells to resemble leaves.
• Serve immediately.

MAKE-AHEAD TIP: Filling can be made earlier in the day. Assemble tartlets up to an hour before serving, cover lightly, and refrigerate until needed.

Chocolate Cake with White Chocolate Buttercream Frosting

Yield: 16 servings

¼ cup unsweetened cocoa powder
¼ cup very hot water
⅓ cup unsalted butter, at room temperature
¾ cup plus 1 tablespoon granulated sugar
1 large egg
1 teaspoon vanilla extract
1⅛ cups all-purpose flour
¾ teaspoon baking soda
¼ teaspoon salt
¾ cup whole buttermilk
1 recipe White Chocolate Buttercream
Garnish: fresh edible flowers*

• Preheat oven to 350°.
• Line 3 (8-inch) round cake pans with parchment paper. Spray pans with cooking spray with flour.
• In a small bowl, combine cocoa powder and hot water, stirring until smooth. Let cool.
• In a large mixing bowl, combine butter and sugar. Beat at high speed with a mixer until fluffy, approximately 5 minutes. Add egg, then vanilla, beating until incorporated.
• In a medium bowl, combine flour, baking soda, and salt, whisking well. Add flour mixture and buttermilk alternately in thirds, beginning and ending with flour mixture. Add cocoa mixture, stirring until incorporated. Divide batter evenly among prepared pans.
• Bake until edges begin to pull away from sides and a wooden pick inserted in the centers comes out clean, 12 to 13 minutes. Let cakes cool in pans on wire racks for 10 minutes.
• Turn out cakes onto wire racks, and let cool completely.
• Spread a thick layer of White Chocolate Buttercream onto top of a cake layer. Top with another cake layer. Spread a thick layer of buttercream onto top of second cake layer. Top with remaining cake layer. Spread a thick layer of buttercream onto sides and top of cake.
• Using a bench scraper or icing spatula, remove or scrape away most of buttercream from sides of cake, if desired, to create a "naked cake" look.
• Garnish top of cake with edible flowers, if desired.
• Store cake in an airtight container in the refrigerator until ready to serve, up to a day.

We used edible flowers from Gourmet Sweet Botanicals, gourmetsweetbotanicals.com.

White Chocolate Buttercream

Gluten-free | *Yield: 3 cups*

8 cups confectioners' sugar
2 cups unsalted butter, softened
¼ teaspoon salt
¼ cup whole milk
1 teaspoon vanilla extract
1 (4-ounce) bar white chocolate, such as Baker's, melted according to package instructions

• In a large mixing bowl, combine confectioners' sugar, butter, salt, milk, and vanilla extract. Beat at low speed with a mixer until combined, scraping down sides of bowl as needed. Increase speed to high, and beat until light and fluffy. Add melted white chocolate, beating until incorporated.
• Use immediately.

MAKE-AHEAD TIP: Buttercream can be made a day in advance, placed in an airtight container, and refrigerated until needed. Let come to room temperature, and beat with a mixer at medium speed for 1 minute before using.

Graduation

Chandler

The
MENU

SCONE
Salt and Pepper Scones
Apricot Black Tea

SAVORIES
Diploma Sandwiches
Graduation Cap Sandwiches
Ham and Apricot Pinwheels
*Darjeeling Poobong Estate
Second Flush SFTGFOP*

SWEETS
Boston Cream Pie
Mini Trifles
Strawberry Pie Mini Trifles
Key Lime Pie Mini Trifles
*Abigail's Blend (Boston
Tea Party Ships & Museum)*

*Tea Pairings by Elmwood Inn Fine Teas,
800-765-2139, elmwoodinn.com*

*A celebratory tea with
themed refreshments is
the perfect send-off for
high school or college
graduates before they
enter the next phase of
their lives.*

gently, bring mixture together with hands until a dough forms.

- Turn out dough onto a lightly floured surface. Using a rolling pin, roll dough to a ¾-inch thickness. Using a 2½-inch fluted square cutter, cut 12 scones from dough. Place scones 2 inches apart on prepared baking sheet.
- Brush tops of scones with reserved 2 tablespoons cream mixture. Sprinkle tops of scones with remaining ⅛ teaspoon salt.
- Bake until lightly golden, approximately 20 minutes.
- Serve warm.

For testing purposes, we used Frontier Alder Smoked Salt available at Whole Foods Markets.

RECOMMENDED CONDIMENT:
Goat Cheese Spread (recipe follows)

Goat Cheese Spread
Gluten-free | *Yield: ¾ cup (12 tablespoons)*

½ cup unsalted butter, softened
4 ounces goat cheese, at room temperature
2 tablespoons heavy whipping cream

- In a medium mixing bowl, combine butter, goat cheese, and cream. Beat at medium speed with a mixer until smooth, 1 to 2 minutes.
- Shape mixture into a log, and wrap in wax paper. Refrigerate until set.
- Slice into 12 (1-tablespoon) portions before serving, if desired.

Salt and Pepper Scones
Yield: 12

4 cups all-purpose flour
2 tablespoons granulated sugar
4 teaspoons baking powder
1⅛ teaspoons smoked sea salt*, divided
½ teaspoon freshly ground black pepper
½ cup cold unsalted butter, cut into pieces
1 cup heavy whipping cream
1 cup whole milk, divided

- Preheat oven to 350°.
- Line a rimmed baking sheet with parchment paper.
- In a large bowl, combine flour, sugar, baking powder, 1 teaspoon salt, and pepper, whisking well. Using a pastry blender, cut butter into flour mixture until it resembles coarse crumbs.
- In a liquid-measuring cup, combine cream and milk, stirring well. Reserve 2 tablespoons cream mixture. Add remaining cream mixture to flour mixture, stirring until evenly moist. (If dough seems dry, add more whipping cream, 1 tablespoon at a time.) Working

Diploma Sandwiches
Yield: 18

1 (8-ounce) package cream cheese, softened
¼ cup salted butter, softened
1 tablespoon heavy whipping cream
¼ cup chopped toasted walnuts
¼ cup minced fresh chives
18 slices soft white bread, crusts removed
Garnish: 18 fresh chives

- In a large mixing bowl, combine cream cheese, butter, and cream. Beat at medium speed with a mixer until fluffy. Add walnuts and chopped chives, stirring to combine.
- Using a rolling pin, flatten bread slices to a ⅛-inch thickness. Spread an even layer of filling onto bread slices.

- Starting at a long side, roll up each bread slice to center. Repeat with opposite side (both rolled edges should touch). Tie each with a chive.
- Serve immediately.

MAKE-AHEAD TIP: Cream cheese spread can be made a day ahead, covered, and refrigerated. Tea sandwiches can be assembled a few hours ahead, covered with damp paper towels, placed in a covered container, and refrigerated until serving time.

Graduation Cap Sandwiches
Yield: 12

12 slices pumpernickel bread, frozen
6 (¼-inch-thick) slices Havarti cheese*
12 (¼-inch-thick) slices salami
12 (¼-inch-thick) slices Roma tomatoes
¼ cup mayonnaise
2 teaspoons fresh lemon zest
1 tablespoon fresh lemon juice
Garnish: sliced matchstick carrots and roasted red
    pepper pieces

- Using a 2½-inch square cutter and a 2-inch round cutter, cut 1 square and 1 circle from each frozen bread slice, discarding scraps.
- Using a 2-inch round cutter, cut 2 circles from each cheese slice*, discarding scraps.
- Using a 2-inch round cutter, cut 1 circle from each salami slice, discarding scraps.
- Stack a cheese round, a salami round, and a tomato slice on top of each bread round.
- In a small bowl, combine mayonnaise, lemon zest, and juice, whisking well. Spread a layer of mayonnaise mixture onto each bread square. Place a bread square, mayonnaise side down, on top of each round stack.
- Referring to photo, garnish each bread square with carrots and roasted red pepper, if desired.
- Serve immediately.

*If slices are smaller than 4 inches wide, you will need 12 slices and will cut 1 circle from each.

MAKE-AHEAD TIP: Bread squares and rounds can be prepared a day ahead and stored in a resealable plastic bag at room temperature. Cheese rounds and salami rounds can be prepared a day ahead, placed in an airtight container, and refrigerated until needed. Mayonnaise mixture can be made a day ahead, covered, and refrigerated. Tea sandwiches can be assembled a few hours ahead, covered with damp paper towels, placed in a covered container, and refrigerated until serving time. Garnish just before serving.

make a 1¼-inch-long slit diagonally toward center of square.
• Place a ham piece in center of each dough square.
• Working clockwise on each dough square, fold the point to the right of each slit to the center to make a pinwheel. Press ends of dough together to seal. Place pinwheels 2 inches apart on prepared baking sheets.
• In a small microwave-safe bowl, heat apricot preserves in a microwave oven in 30-second intervals until melted. Add cayenne pepper, stirring well. Brush mixture onto pinwheels.
• Bake until lightly golden, 8 to 10 minutes. Let cool slightly on baking sheets before serving.

MAKE-AHEAD TIP: Pinwheels can be assembled an hour in advance, placed on prepared baking sheets, draped with damp paper towels, covered with plastic wrap, and refrigerated. Brush with apricot mixture just before baking.

Boston Cream Pie Mini Trifles
Yield: 14

½ cup salted butter, softened
1¼ cups granulated sugar
½ vanilla bean, scraped and seeds reserved
2 large eggs
2 cups cake flour
2 teaspoons baking powder
½ teaspoon salt
¾ cup whole milk
1 recipe Vanilla Bean Custard (recipe follows)
1 recipe Chocolate Ganache (recipe follows)

• Preheat oven to 350°.
• Spray a (15x10x1-inch) jelly-roll pan with cooking spray. Line with parchment paper. Spray again.
• In a large mixing bowl, combine butter, sugar, and reserved vanilla bean seeds. Beat at medium-high speed with a mixer until fluffy, approximately 3 minutes. Add eggs, one at a time, beating well after each addition.
• In a large bowl, combine cake flour, baking powder, and salt, sifting well. Gradually add to butter mixture alternately with milk, beginning and ending with flour mixture. Pour batter into prepared pan.
• Bake until lightly golden, approximately 16 minutes. Let cool completely in pan.
• Using a 1¾-inch round cutter, cut 28 circles from cake, discarding scraps.
• In 14 (2-inch-wide) trifle dishes, layer a cake round, half of Vanilla Bean Custard, and half of Chocolate Ganache. Repeat layers with remaining ingredients.
• Serve immediately, or cover and refrigerate for up to 2 hours.

Ham and Apricot Pinwheels
Yield: 24

1 (17.3-ounce) package frozen puff pastry (2 sheets), thawed
24 (1-inch-square, ¼-inch-thick) pieces ham
¼ cup apricot preserves
⅛ teaspoon ground cayenne pepper

• Preheat oven to 400°.
• Line several baking sheets with parchment paper.
• On a lightly floured surface, unfold puff pastry. Using a rolling pin, roll out each sheet to a 14x11-inch rectangle. Cut each sheet into 12 (3-inch) squares.
• Beginning at each corner point of dough squares,

Vanilla-Bean Custard

Gluten-free | *Yield: approximately 2½ cups*

2½ cups whole milk
½ vanilla bean, split, scraped, and seeds reserved
6 egg yolks
⅔ cup granulated sugar
3 tablespoons cornstarch
¼ teaspoon salt

• In a large saucepan, combine milk and reserved vanilla bean seeds. Scald milk over medium-high heat.
• In a large bowl, combine egg yolks, sugar, cornstarch, and salt, whisking well to combine. Slowly add scalded milk, whisking well.
• Return mixture to saucepan. Bring to a boil for 1 minute over medium heat, whisking continuously. Remove from heat.

• Transfer custard to a heatproof container. Place plastic wrap on the surface of custard to prevent it from forming a skin while cooling.
• Refrigerate until very cold, 4 to 6 hours, before using.

Chocolate Ganache

Gluten-free | *Yield: approximately 1 cup*

8 ounces semisweet chocolate, coarsely chopped
½ cup heavy whipping cream
2 tablespoons light corn syrup
2 tablespoons unsalted butter

• In a medium microwave-safe bowl, combine chocolate, cream, corn syrup, and butter. Microwave on high in 30-second intervals until melted, stirring between each interval.
• Let cool to room temperature before using.

- Using a 1½-inch triangular cutter, cut 14 triangles from pie dough, and arrange in open spaces on prepared baking sheets.
- Bake pie dough and triangles until golden brown, approximately 10 minutes. Let cool completely on baking sheets.
- Reserving triangles for garnish, break remaining piecrust into large pieces.
- In a medium bowl, combine sliced strawberries and remaining ¼ cup sugar.
- In 14 miniature trifle dishes, layer half of piecrust pieces, 1 cup strawberries, 1¼ cups Whipped Cream, remaining half of piecrust pieces, and remaining 1½ cups strawberries.
- Place remaining 1 cup Whipped Cream in a piping bag fitted with a large open-star tip (Wilton #1M). Pipe a rosette onto each trifle.
- Top each trifle with a reserved piecrust triangle.
- Garnish each trifle with a strawberry slice and a mint sprig, if desired.
- Serve immediately.

MAKE-AHEAD TIP: Piecrust can be prepared a day ahead and stored in an airtight container at room temperature.

Whipped Cream
Gluten-free | *Yield: approximately 4½ cups*

3 cups heavy whipping cream
1 cup confectioners' sugar
½ tablespoon vanilla extract

- In a large mixing bowl, beat whipping cream at high speed with a mixer until soft peaks form. Gradually add confectioners' sugar and vanilla extract, beating until stiff peaks form.
- Refrigerate until needed, up to 2 hours.

Strawberry Pie Mini Trifles
Yield: 14

1 (14.1-ounce) package refrigerated pie dough (2 sheets)
1 egg white
1 tablespoon water
¼ cup plus 2 tablespoons granulated sugar, divided
2½ cups sliced strawberries
2¼ cups Whipped Cream (recipe follows), divided
Garnish: 14 slices strawberry and 14 sprigs fresh mint

- Preheat oven to 425°.
- Line 2 rimmed baking sheets with parchment paper.
- Unroll 1 pie dough sheet on each baking sheet.
- In a small bowl, combine egg white and water, whisking well. Brush onto pie dough. Sprinkle pie dough with 2 tablespoons sugar.

Key Lime Pie Mini Trifles
Yield: 14

1 (8-ounce) package cream cheese, softened
1 (14-ounce) can sweetened condensed milk
⅓ cup bottled Key lime juice
1 tablespoon fresh lime zest
1 drop green food coloring (optional)
2 cups graham cracker crumbs
¼ cup granulated sugar
2¼ cups Whipped Cream (recipe above), divided
Garnish: 4 thin slices lime cut into quarters

- In a medium mixing bowl, combine cream cheese, condensed milk, Key lime juice, and lime zest. Beat at

medium speed with a mixer until smooth. Tint mixture with food coloring, if desired.

• In another medium bowl, combine graham cracker crumbs and sugar, stirring well.

• In 14 miniature trifle dishes, layer ¾ cup graham-cracker mixture, half of cream cheese mixture, 1¼ cups Whipped Cream, ¾ cup graham-cracker mixture, remaining half of cream cheese mixture, and remaining ¾ cup graham-cracker mixture.

• Place remaining 1 cup Whipped Cream in a piping bag fitted with a large open-star tip (Wilton #1M). Pipe a rosette onto each trifle.

• Garnish each trifle with a lime slice quarter, if desired.

• Serve immediately.

MAKE-AHEAD TIP: Trifles can be assembled an hour ahead, covered, and refrigerated. Pipe cream rosettes, and garnish just before serving.

Engagement

The
MENU

SCONE
Toasted Coconut Scones
*Chardonnay Meursault
Tea Blend*

SAVORIES
Cucumber Flower Canapés
Crab and Gruyère Quiche
Green Salad with
Sherry-Shallot Vinaigrette
Mojito Green Tea

SWEETS
Raspberry-Macadamia
French Macarons
Lemon-Pistachio Tartlets
Peach-Ginger Shortcakes
Love at First Sip Black Tea

*Tea Pairings by Carriage House Tea,
carriagehousetea.com*

*Monogrammed dishes
and décor—whether new
or family heirlooms—
are splendid details
to congratulate the
upcoming nuptials of a
newly engaged couple.*

Toasted Coconut Scones
Yield: 21

2 cups all-purpose flour
⅓ cup sweetened flaked coconut, finely chopped
  and toasted*
¼ cup granulated sugar
2 teaspoons baking powder
½ teaspoon salt
4 tablespoons cold salted butter, cut into pieces
¾ cup cold canned coconut milk, such as Goya
2 tablespoons heavy whipping cream

• Preheat oven to 450°.
• Line a rimmed baking sheet with parchment paper.
• In a large bowl, combine flour, toasted coconut, sugar, baking powder, and salt, whisking well. Using a pastry blender, cut butter into flour mixture until it resembles coarse crumbs. Add coconut milk, stirring until mixture is evenly moist. (If dough seems dry, add more coconut milk, 1 tablespoon at a time.) Working gently, bring mixture together with hands until a dough forms.
• Turn out dough onto a lightly floured surface. Knead gently 3 to 4 times. Using a rolling pin, roll dough to a ½-inch thickness. Using a 1¼-inch fluted square cutter, cut 21 scones from dough. Place scones 2 inches apart on prepared baking sheet. Brush tops of scones with cream.
• Bake until edges of scones are golden brown and a wooden pick inserted in the centers comes out clean, 6 to 8 minutes.
• Serve warm.

Pulse coconut in a food processor until finely chopped, and then toast.

RECOMMENDED CONDIMENTS:
Clotted Cream
Pineapple Jam

Cucumber Flower Canapés
Yield: 16

⅓ cup mayonnaise
1 teaspoon sweet onion, finely chopped
1 teaspoon fresh lemon zest
1 teaspoon fresh lemon juice
⅛ teaspoon salt
⅛ teaspoon ground black pepper
8 slices firm white sandwich bread, frozen
64 paper-thin slices English cucumber with peel*
Garnish: fresh lemon zest

Cucumber Flower
How-Tos
ON PAGE 128

• In a small bowl, combine mayonnaise, onion, lemon zest, lemon juice, salt, and pepper, whisking to blend. Cover and refrigerate for 1 hour to allow flavors to meld.

• Using a 1¾-inch square cutter, cut 16 shapes from frozen bread.

• Spread ¼ teaspoon mayonnaise mixture onto each bread square. Fold each cucumber slice in half and then in quarters. Pinch the inner fold of each cucumber slice between thumb and forefinger, and place on bread square, green edges up. Repeat 3 times per canapé. Arrange folds to resemble a flower.

• Garnish cucumber flowers with lemon zest in centers, if desired.

• Serve immediately, or refrigerate, lightly covered, for up to 30 minutes before serving.

*A mandoline is essential for cutting paper-thin slices of cucumber. For testing purposes, we used a Kyocera mandoline, available at Sur la Table, surlatable.com.

Crab and Gruyère Quiche

Yield: 8 servings

½ (14.1-ounce) package refrigerated pie dough
  (1 sheet)
1¼ cups heavy whipping cream
3 large eggs
¼ cup finely chopped red bell pepper
2 tablespoons finely chopped parsley
2 tablespoons finely chopped fresh chives
1 tablespoon fresh lemon zest
½ teaspoon salt
¼ teaspoon ground black pepper
⅛ teaspoon ground nutmeg
2 cups coarsely shredded Gruyère cheese
¾ cup jumbo lump crabmeat

• Preheat oven to 450°.
• Unroll pie dough, and press into a 9-inch tart pan with a removable bottom, trimming excess as necessary. Using the wide end of a chopstick, push pie dough into indentations in sides of tart pan. Refrigerate for 30 minutes.
• Prick bottom of pie dough with a fork to prevent puffing while baking.
• Bake until crust is light golden brown, 5 to 7 minutes. Let cool completely.
• Reduce oven temperature to 350°.
• In a medium bowl, combine cream, eggs, red bell pepper, parsley, chives, lemon zest, salt, pepper, and nutmeg, whisking to blend.
• Evenly sprinkle cheese on baked crust. Arrange crab evenly over cheese. Pour egg mixture over crab and cheese layers.
• Bake until quiche is set and slightly puffed, 38 to 40 minutes. Let cool in pan for 15 minutes. Remove quiche from tart pan before cutting and serving.

Green Salad with Sherry-Shallot Vinaigrette

Gluten-free | *Yield: 8 servings*

7 to 9 spears fresh asparagus
¼ teaspoon olive oil
8 cups mixed baby lettuces
½ cup coarsely grated carrots
½ cup chopped canned artichoke hearts
½ cup sliced yellow and red grape tomatoes
1 recipe Sherry-Shallot Vinaigrette (recipe follows)

• Preheat oven to 400°.
• Line a rimmed baking sheet with parchment paper.
• Snap off tough ends of asparagus, and discard. Toss asparagus spears in olive oil. Place on prepared baking sheet.
• Bake asparagus until crisp-tender, approximately 5 to 7 minutes. Let cool slightly, and chop into ¾-inch lengths. (You should have approximately ½ cup roasted asparagus.)
• In a large bowl, combine lettuces, carrots, asparagus, artichoke hearts, and tomatoes, tossing well.
• Serve with Sherry-Shallot Vinaigrette.

MAKE-AHEAD TIP: Salad can be made earlier in the day, covered, and refrigerated.

Sherry-Shallot Vinaigrette

Gluten-free | *Yield: ¾ cup*

3 tablespoons sherry vinegar
1 tablespoon very finely minced shallot
1 tablespoon fresh lemon juice
1 teaspoon granulated sugar
1 teaspoon Dijon-style mustard
¼ teaspoon salt
⅛ teaspoon ground black pepper
½ cup extra-virgin olive oil

• In a small bowl, combine vinegar, shallot, lemon juice, sugar, mustard, salt, and pepper, stirring to blend. Let stand for 15 minutes.
• Add olive oil in a slow steady stream, whisking vigorously until ingredients are emulsified.

KITCHEN TIP: If a whisk is not available, place ingredients for Sherry-Shallot Vinaigrette in a jar with a tight-fitting lid, and shake until combined.

MAKE-AHEAD TIP: Sherry-Shallot Vinaigrette can be made a day in advance, covered, and refrigerated. Let come to room temperature before serving, and whisk to remix.

Raspberry-Macadamia French Macarons

Gluten-free | *Yield: 18*

3 large egg whites
1½ cups salted macadamia nuts
1½ cups confectioners' sugar, divided
2 tablespoons granulated sugar
⅓ cup seedless raspberry jam

• Place egg whites in a large mixing bowl, and let stand, uncovered, at room temperature for exactly 3 hours. (Aging egg whites in this manner is essential to creating perfect macarons.)
• Line 2 rimmed baking sheets with parchment paper. Using a pencil, draw 2-inch circles 2 inches apart on parchment paper. Turn parchment paper over.
• In the work bowl of a food processor, combine macadamia nuts and 2 tablespoons confectioners' sugar, pulsing just to combine. (Don't overprocess or a nut butter will be created. Nut particles should stay separate and dry, not clump together.) Add remaining confectioners' sugar, and process just until combined.
• Beat egg whites at medium-high speed with a mixer until frothy. Gradually add granulated sugar, beating at high speed until stiff peaks form, approximately 5 minutes. (Egg whites will be creamy, shiny, and thick.)

Add macadamia-nut mixture to egg whites, folding until well combined. (Batter should fall off spatula in thick ribbons.) Let batter stand for 15 minutes.
• Transfer batter to a pastry bag fitted with a medium round tip (Wilton #12). Pipe batter into drawn circles on prepared baking sheets.
• Slam baking sheets vigorously on countertop 5 to 7 times to release air bubbles. Let stand at room temperature for 45 to 60 minutes before baking to help develop macaron's signature crisp exterior when baked. (Macarons should feel dry to the touch and not stick to the finger.)
• Preheat oven to 275°.
• Bake until macarons are firm to the touch, approximately 24 minutes. Let cool completely on pans.
• Place raspberry jam in a piping bag fitted with a medium round tip (Wilton #12), and pipe jam onto flat side of half of macarons. Top each with another macaron, flat sides together. Push down lightly, and twist so jam spreads to edges.
• Serve immediately.

MAKE-AHEAD TIP: Wrap unfilled macarons in plastic wrap in groups to prevent crushing or breaking. Transfer to airtight containers. Refrigerate for up to 2 days until needed. Let come to room temperature before filling and serving.

> *"The love we give away*
> *is the only love we keep."*
>
> —ELBERT HUBBARD

Lemon-Pistachio Tartlets
Yield: 12

1 (14.1-ounce) package refrigerated pie dough
  (2 sheets)
1 large egg
½ cup firmly packed light brown sugar
3 tablespoons light corn syrup
1 tablespoon salted butter, melted
1 teaspoon fresh lemon zest
½ teaspoon vanilla extract
½ teaspoon lemon extract
¾ cup very finely chopped, roasted, salted pistachios
Garnish: lemon zest curls

- Preheat oven to 450°.
- Lightly spray 12 (4x2¼-inch) diamond-shaped tartlet pans with cooking spray.
- Unroll pie dough on a lightly floured surface. Using a tartlet pan as a guide, cut 12 shapes from pie dough. Press dough into prepared tartlet pans, discarding excess dough. Using a chopstick, push pie dough into indentations in sides of tartlet pans. Place prepared tartlet pans on a rimmed baking sheet. Refrigerate for 30 minutes.
- Prick bottoms of pie dough with a fork to prevent puffing during baking.
- Bake until tartlet shells are very light golden brown, 5 to 7 minutes. Let cool completely in pans.
- Reduce oven to 350°.
- In a medium bowl, combine egg, brown sugar, corn syrup, melted butter, lemon zest, vanilla extract, and lemon extract, whisking to blend. Add pistachios, stirring to combine. Divide mixture evenly among baked tartlet shells, filling each one three-fourths full.
- Bake until filling is set and puffed, 13 to 15 minutes. (Filling will fall as it cools.) Let tartlets cool completely before removing from pans.
- Garnish each with a lemon curl, if desired.

KITCHEN TIP: Pistachios in the shell tend to be a brighter green than shelled pistachios. To give these tartlets their best color, we recommend buying pistachios in the shell and shelling your own.

Tartlet Crust
How-Tos
ON PAGE 130

- Preheat oven to 350°.
- Line a rimmed baking sheet with parchment paper.
- In a large bowl, combine flour, ⅓ cup sugar, crystalized ginger, baking powder, ground ginger, and salt, whisking well. Using a pastry blender, cut butter into flour mixture until mixture resembles coarse crumbs.
- In a liquid-measuring cup, combine ¾ cup cream and vanilla extract, stirring to blend. Add to flour mixture, stirring until mixture is evenly moist. (If dough seems dry, add more cream, 1 tablespoon at a time.) Working gently, bring mixture together with hands until a dough forms.
- Turn out dough onto a lightly floured surface. Knead gently 3 to 4 times. Using a rolling pin, roll dough to a ½-inch thickness. Using a 2-inch fluted round cutter, cut 13 shortcakes from dough. Place shortcakes 2 inches apart on prepared baking sheet, and brush tops of shortcakes with remaining 2 tablespoons cream.
- Bake until edges are golden brown and a wooden pick inserted in the centers comes out clean, approximately 18 minutes. Let shortcakes cool on baking sheet.
- In a medium bowl, combine peaches, remaining 1 tablespoon sugar, and lemon juice, tossing to coat. Let stand for 15 minutes to mascerate.
- Using a serrated knife, cut shortcakes in half horizontally.
- Place Sweetened Whipped Cream in a piping bag fitted with a large open-star tip (Wilton #1). Pipe a swirl of whipped cream onto bottom halves of shortcakes. Place 2 tablespoons peaches each on top of cream. Top each with top halves of shortcakes. Pipe a rosette of whipped cream on top of each shortcake.
- Garnish each shortcake with a peach slice and a mint sprig, if desired.
- Serve immediately.

MAKE-AHEAD TIP: Shortcakes can be made a day in advance and stored at room temperature in an airtight container until needed. Reheat in a 350° oven for 5 minutes before cutting and filling.

Peach-Ginger Shortcakes
Yield: 13

2 cups all-purpose flour
⅓ cup plus 1 tablespoon granulated sugar, divided
2 tablespoons finely chopped crystalized ginger
2½ teaspoons baking powder
2 teaspoons ground ginger
½ teaspoon salt
4 tablespoons cold butter, cut into pieces
¾ cup plus 2 tablespoons cold heavy whipping cream, divided
½ teaspoon vanilla extract
1½ cups diced, peeled peaches
1 tablespoon fresh lemon juice
1 recipe Sweetened Whipped Cream (recipe follows)
Garnish: fresh peach slices and fresh mint

Sweetened Whipped Cream
Yield: 2 cups

1½ cups cold heavy whipping cream
¼ cup confectioners' sugar
½ teaspoon vanilla extract

- In a large mixing bowl, combine cream, confectioners' sugar, and vanilla extract. Beat at high speed with a mixer until stiff peaks form. Cover, and refrigerate until needed.

Bridal
SHOWER

The MENU

SCONE
Hazelnut-Allspice Scones
Black Currant Black Tea

SAVORIES
Port Salut and Fig
Phyllo Cups

Pork and Mushroom
Puff Pastry Swirls

Smoked Turkey and
Brussels Sprouts Slaw
Tea Sandwiches
Lover's Leap Black Tea

SWEETS
Butterscotch-Pecan
Shortbread Sandwich Cookies

Blackberry Mousse
Sponge Cakes

Goat Cheese, Lavender,
and Honey
Mini Cheesecakes
Da Hong Pao Oolong Tea

Tea Pairings by Global Tea Mart,
844-208-2337, globalteamart.com

Fresh flowers, pretty
china, and dainty treats
create an idyllic setting to
honor the bride before her
walk down the aisle.

Hazelnut-Allspice Scones
Yield: 18

2 cups all-purpose flour
⅓ cup plus 2 tablespoons granulated sugar
2 teaspoons baking powder
1 teaspoon ground allspice
½ teaspoon salt
4 tablespoons cold salted butter, cut into pieces
½ cup chopped toasted hazelnuts
¾ cup plus 3 tablespoons cold heavy whipping
　cream, divided
½ teaspoon vanilla extract

• Preheat oven to 350°.
• Line a rimmed baking sheet with parchment paper.
• In a large bowl, combine flour, sugar, baking powder, allspice, and salt, whisking well. Using a pastry blender, cut butter into flour mixture until it resembles coarse crumbs. Add nuts, stirring to combine.
• In a liquid-measuring cup, combine ¾ cup plus 2 tablespoons cream and vanilla extract, whisking to blend. Add to flour mixture, stirring until evenly moist. (If dough seems dry, add more cream, 1 tablespoon at a time.) Working gently, bring mixture together with hands until a dough forms.
• Turn out dough onto a lightly floured surface. Knead lightly 4 to 5 times. Using a rolling pin, roll dough to a ½-inch thickness. Using a 2-inch square cutter, cut 18 scones from dough, rerolling scraps as necessary. Place scones 2 inches apart on prepared baking sheet. Brush tops of scones with remaining 1 tablespoon cream.
• Bake until scones are light golden brown and a wooden pick inserted in the centers comes out clean, 18 to 20 minutes.
• Serve warm.

RECOMMENDED CONDIMENT:
Clotted Cream

Port Salut and Fig Phyllo Cups
Yield: 15

1 (1.9-ounce) package mini phyllo shells (15 shells),
　such as Athens
3 ounces Port Salut cheese*
8 teaspoons fig preserves
Garnish: fresh rosemary

• Preheat oven to 350°.
• Line a rimmed baking sheet with parchment paper.
• Place phyllo shells on prepared baking sheet.

- Cut cheese into 15 equal pieces. Place a piece of cheese in each phyllo shell.
- Bake only until cheese melts, 3 to 5 minutes. Immediately divide fig preserves among phyllo cups, covering cheese.
- Garnish with rosemary, if desired.
- Serve immediately.

Port Salut is a mild, soft French cheese. If not available, another cheese, such as Brie, may be substituted.

Pork and Mushroom Puff Pastry Swirls
Yield: 22

1 cup sliced white button mushrooms
3 teaspoons olive oil, divided
¼ teaspoon salt
1 pound ground pork
¼ teaspoon garlic salt
⅛ teaspoon ground black pepper
¼ cup chopped yellow bell pepper
¼ cup chopped sweet onion
1 (17.3-ounce) package frozen puff pastry (2 sheets)
1 tablespoon fresh thyme leaves
1 large egg
1 tablespoon water
¼ cup honey
¼ cup spicy brown mustard
Garnish: fresh thyme sprigs

- Preheat oven to 350°.
- Line 2 rimmed baking sheets with parchment paper.
- In a medium bowl, toss mushrooms with 2 teaspoons olive oil. Spread mushrooms in a single layer on a prepared baking sheet, and sprinkle with salt.
- Bake until mushrooms are tender and have released their liquid, 20 to 25 minutes. Let cool on baking sheet, and chop finely.

- In a large nonstick sauté pan, heat remaining 1 teaspoon olive oil over medium-high heat. Add pork, breaking apart into crumbles. Add garlic salt and black pepper. Add yellow bell pepper and onion, stirring and cooking until pork is browned and vegetables are tender, approximately 5 minutes. Drain pork mixture on paper towels. Transfer pork mixture to a bowl. Add mushrooms, stirring to combine. Let cool.
- Increase oven temperature to 400°.
- Let puff pastry thaw just enough to be able to roll up and encase filling. (It should still be cold and firm.)
- Unroll both sheets on a lightly floured surface. Using a rolling pin, roll out puff pastry until smooth. Divide pork mixture evenly between puff pastry sheets, leaving a 1-inch margin around edges and pressing mixture lightly into pastry. Sprinkle each evenly with thyme leaves. Starting at a long end, roll up pastry firmly and evenly to encase ingredients and form a cylinder. Tuck ends under.
- Using a serrated knife in a sawing motion, cut 11 (½-inch) slices from each cylinder. Place slices 2 inches apart on remaining prepared baking sheet.
- In a small bowl, combine egg and water, whisking to blend. Brush slices with egg mixture.
- Bake until golden brown, approximately 15 minutes.
- In a small bowl, combine honey and mustard, stirring until blended. Brush warm pastries with honey mixture.
- Garnish with thyme sprigs, if desired.
- Serve immediately.

MAKE-AHEAD TIP: Puff pastry can be assembled a day in advance, and cylinder can be wrapped in plastic wrap and refrigerated. Just before serving, unwrap, slice, brush with egg mixture, and bake.

- In a medium bowl, combine Brussels sprouts, carrot, onion, and cranberries, tossing well.
- In a small bowl, combine vinegar, sugar, salt, and pepper, whisking well. Add olive oil in a slow, steady stream, whisking until emulsified. Add vinaigrette to slaw, stirring until combined. Refrigerate for 4 hours to meld flavors.
- Using a serrated bread knife, trim and discard crusts from bread slices. Cut each slice into 2 (4x2-inch) rectangles. Cover with damp paper towels, and set aside.
- Cut turkey slices into 7x2-inch pieces.
- Place pieces from 1 turkey slice on each of 12 bread rectangles, ruffling and gathering turkey to fit. Top each evenly with slaw. Top with remaining bread rectangles.
- Serve immediately, or cover with damp paper towels, place in a covered container, and refrigerate for up to an hour.

MAKE-AHEAD TIP: Slaw can be made a day in advance, covered, and refrigerated. Bread slices can be cut a day in advance and stored at room temperature in a resealable plastic bag.

Butterscotch-Pecan Shortbread Sandwich Cookies
Yield: 24

1¾ cups all-purpose flour
¼ teaspoon salt
¾ cup salted butter, softened
½ cup granulated sugar
¾ teaspoon vanilla extract
½ cup finely chopped toasted pecans
1 recipe Butterscotch Ganache (recipe follows)

- Preheat oven to 350°.
- Line 2 rimmed baking sheets with parchment paper.
- In a medium bowl, combine flour and salt, whisking well.
- In a large mixing bowl, combine butter and sugar. Beat at medium speed with a mixer until light and creamy. Add vanilla extract, beating until incorporated. Add flour mixture, beating until a dough forms. Add pecans, beating to combine.
- Wrap dough tightly in plastic wrap. Refrigerate for 1 hour.
- Turn out dough onto a lightly floured surface. Using a rolling pin, roll dough to a ¼-inch thickness. Using a 1¾-inch fluted round cutter, cut 48 cookies from dough, rerolling scraps as necessary. Place cookies 2 inches apart on prepared baking sheets. Freeze for 15 minutes.

Smoked Turkey and Brussels Sprouts Slaw Tea Sandwiches
Yield: 12

2 cups whole fresh Brussels sprouts, very finely chopped
2 tablespoons finely shredded carrot
2 tablespoons finely chopped purple onion
2 tablespoons chopped dried cranberries
2 tablespoons apple cider vinegar
1 teaspoon granulated sugar
¼ teaspoon salt
¼ teaspoon ground black pepper
2 tablespoons olive oil
12 slices whole-wheat bread
12 ultrathin slices deli smoked turkey

- Bake until edges are just lightly golden brown, 11 to 13 minutes. Transfer to wire racks. Let cool completely.
- Place Butterscotch Ganache in a resealable plastic bag*, and snip off one corner. Pipe filling evenly onto bottoms (flat sides) of 24 cookies, and top each with another cookie, flat side down. Twist cookies to spread ganache to the edges.
- Place cookies in an airtight container with layers separated by wax paper, and refrigerate until needed. Let come to room temperature before serving.

*You may also use a piping bag fitted with a medium round tip.

Butterscotch Ganache
Gluten-free | Yield: ¾ cup

1 cup butterscotch morsels
¼ cup heavy whipping cream

- In the top half of a double boiler over simmering water, combine butterscotch morsels and cream. Cook, stirring occasionally, until morsels melt and mixture is smooth. Let cool slightly before using.

MAKE-AHEAD TIP: Cookies can be baked a week in advance, placed in an airtight container, and frozen. Let thaw completely before filling with Butterscotch Ganache.

"The best thing to hold onto in life is each other." —AUDREY HEPBURN

Blackberry Mousse Sponge Cakes
Yield: 11

1 cup granulated sugar
1 teaspoon fresh orange zest
1 cup sifted cake flour, such as Swans Down
1 teaspoon baking powder
¼ teaspoon salt
3 large eggs, separated, at room temperature
¼ cup very hot water
1¼ teaspoons vanilla extract
1 recipe Blackberry Mousse (recipe follows)
Garnish: orange peel curls

• Preheat oven to 350°.
• Spray an 18x13-inch rimmed baking sheet with cooking spray. Line with parchment paper, and spray again.
• In a small bowl, combine sugar and orange zest, whisking well.
• In another small bowl, combine cake flour, baking powder, and salt, whisking well.
• In a large mixing bowl, beat egg yolks at high speed with a mixer until very light. Gradually add sugar mixture, beating to combine. Add hot water and vanilla extract, beating until incorporated. Gradually add flour mixture, beating until incorporated.
• In another mixing bowl, beat egg whites at high speed with a mixer until stiff peaks form. Add to cake batter, folding gently until combined. Spread batter into prepared pan, smoothing to create a level surface.
• Bake until edges are light golden brown and a wooden pick inserted in the center of cake comes out clean, approximately 10 minutes. Let cake cool completely in pan.
• Using a 2-inch round cutter, cut 33 circles from cake.
• Place Blackberry Mousse in a piping bag fitted with a large open-star tip (Wilton #1). Pipe mousse decoratively onto 11 cake circles. Top each with another cake circle, and pipe with mousse. Repeat with remaining cake circles and mousse.
• Garnish each with an orange peel curl, if desired.

Blackberry Mousse
Gluten-free | *Yield: 2 cups*

1½ cups cold heavy whipping cream
3 to 4 tablespoons seedless blackberry preserves

• In a large mixing bowl, beat cream at high speed with a mixer until thickened. Add preserves,

1 tablespoon at a time, until desired color is achieved.
• Cover and refrigerate until needed.

MAKE-AHEAD TIP: Cake can be baked a day in advance. Rounds can be cut and stored in an airtight container at room temperature. Blackberry Mousse can be made earlier in the day, placed in a covered container, and refrigerated until needed. Cakes can be assembled, covered, and refrigerated for up to 1 hour before serving.

Goat Cheese, Lavender, and Honey Mini Cheesecakes
Yield: 12

¾ cup graham cracker crumbs
⅓ cup plus 1 tablespoon granulated sugar, divided
3 tablespoons salted butter, melted
4 ounces cream cheese, at room temperature
4 ounces goat cheese, at room temperature
1 tablespoon heavy whipping cream
3 tablespoons all-purpose flour
½ teaspoon vanilla extract
1 large egg
½ teaspoon culinary lavender, such as McCormick's
Garnish: honey and fresh lavender blossoms

• Preheat oven to 350°.
• Lightly spray a 12-well mini cheesecake pan with removable bottoms with cooking spray.
• In a small bowl, combine graham cracker crumbs, 1 tablespoon sugar, and melted butter, stirring to blend. Divide crumb mixture evenly among wells of prepared pan, pressing firmly to create a level base.
• Bake until light golden brown, 6 to 8 minutes. Let cool completely.
• In a medium mixing bowl, combine cream cheese, goat cheese, and cream. Beat at medium speed with a mixer until smooth. Add remaining ⅓ cup sugar, flour, and vanilla extract, beating until incorporated. Add egg and lavender, beating until incorporated. Divide mixture evenly among wells of prepared pan.
• Bake until cheesecakes are set and slightly puffed, 10 to 11 minutes. Let cool completely.
• Wrap pan well with plastic wrap. Refrigerate for at least 8 hours.
• Remove cheesecakes from pan.
• Garnish each with a drizzle of honey and with fresh lavender blossoms, if desired.
• Serve immediately.

The
MENU

SCONE
Blueberry-Thyme Scones
Lemon Meringue Rooibos

SAVORIES
Pimiento Cheese
Triple Stacks
Ham and Broccoli Slaw
Tea Sandwiches
Tomato-Dill Shortbreads
with Olive Salad
North Point Darjeeling

SWEETS
White Chocolate Blondies
Lemon-Basil Cookies
Strawberry Bundt Cake
Strawberry Mini Bundt Cakes
Jasmine Green Tea

Tea Pairings by Trail Lodge Tea,
314-680-3015, traillodgetea.com

Serve a classic afternoon-
tea menu in a timeless,
stylish setting to honor a
milestone birthday with
close friends. ❧

- In a large bowl, combine flour, sugar, thyme, baking powder, lemon zest, and salt, whisking well. Using a pastry blender, cut butter into flour mixture until it resembles coarse crumbs.
- In a liquid-measuring cup, combine cream and vanilla extract, stirring to blend. Add to flour mixture, stirring until mixture is evenly moist. (If dough seems dry, add more cream, 1 tablespoon at a time.) Working gently, bring mixture together with hands until a dough forms.
- Turn out dough onto a lightly floured surface. Knead gently 3 to 4 times. Using a rolling pin, roll dough to a ½-inch thickness. Scatter ¼ cup blueberries on half of dough. Fold other half of dough over blueberries to enclose them. Lightly roll out dough again to a ½-inch thickness. Repeat scattering, folding, and rolling process with remaining ¼ cup blueberries.
- Using a 2¼-inch round cutter, cut 11 scones from dough, rerolling scraps as necessary. Place scones 2 inches apart on prepared baking sheet.
- Bake until edges are light golden brown and a wooden pick inserted in the centers comes out clean, 10 to 11 minutes.

RECOMMENDED CONDIMENTS:
Clotted Cream
Lemon Curd

Pimiento Cheese Triple Stacks
Yield: 9

4 ounces goat cheese, at room temperature
1 teaspoon heavy whipping cream
1½ cups shredded Colby-Jack cheese
1 (4-ounce) jar diced pimientos, drained
⅓ cup mayonnaise
½ teaspoon Worcestershire sauce
⅛ teaspoon ground black pepper
⅛ teaspoon ground red pepper
9 slices very thin whole-wheat bread

- In a medium mixing bowl, combine goat cheese and cream. Beat at high speed with a mixer until smooth. Add Colby-Jack cheese and pimientos, stirring to combine.
- In a small bowl, combine mayonnaise, Worcestershire sauce, black pepper, and red pepper, whisking well. Add to cheese mixture, stirring until incorporated. Cover, and refrigerate until needed, up to a day.
- Spread approximately 3 tablespoons pimiento cheese each onto 3 bread slices. Top each with another bread slice. Spread another 3 tablespoons pimiento cheese on top. Top each with a third bread slice.

Blueberry-Thyme Scones
Yield: 11

2 cups soft winter-wheat all-purpose flour,
    such as White Lily
¼ cup granulated sugar
2 tablespoons fresh thyme leaves
2 teaspoons baking powder
2 teaspoons fresh lemon zest
½ teaspoon salt
5 tablespoons cold unsalted butter, cut into pieces
¾ cup cold heavy whipping cream
¼ teaspoon vanilla extract
½ cup fresh blueberries, divided

- Preheat oven to 400°.
- Line a rimmed baking sheet with parchment paper.

• Using a serrated bread knife, trim and discard crusts from sandwiches. Cut 3 finger sandwiches from each whole sandwich.
• Serve immediately.

KITCHEN TIP: *For pretty tea sandwiches, use a sharp serrated bread knife, and wipe knife after each cut.*

Ham and Broccoli Slaw Tea Sandwiches
Yield: 24

12 slices white sandwich bread, frozen
¼ cup mayonnaise
2 teaspoons apple cider vinegar
2 teaspoons granulated sugar
¼ teaspoon salt
⅛ teaspoon ground black pepper
2 cups finely chopped broccoli florets
¼ cup finely grated carrot
1½ teaspoons finely chopped shallot
12 slices ultrathin deli ham

• Using a 1¾-inch round cutter, cut 24 rounds from frozen bread slices, discarding scraps. Cover bread rounds with damp paper towels, or place in a resealable plastic bag to prevent drying out.
• In a small bowl, combine mayonnaise, vinegar, sugar, salt, and pepper, whisking well.
• In a medium bowl, combine broccoli, carrot, and shallot, tossing to blend. Add mayonnaise mixture, stirring to combine. Cover, and refrigerate until needed, up to a day.
• Cut ham into 24 (5x2-inch) pieces. Place 1 ham piece on each of 12 bread rounds, gathering ham into ruffled circles. Top each with 1 teaspoon slaw and another bread round. Secure with a decorative frilled pick, if desired.
• Serve immediately.

MAKE-AHEAD TIP: *Bread rounds can be cut a day in advance and stored in a resealable plastic bag. Slaw can be made earlier in the day. Sandwiches can be assembled, covered with damp paper towels, and refrigerated for up to 1 hour before serving.*

- Just before serving, place ½ teaspoon Olive Salad on each shortbread.

MAKE-AHEAD TIP: Shortbreads can be made a week in advance, stored in an airtight container, and frozen. Let thaw completely before topping with Olive Salad.

Olive Salad
Gluten-free | *Yield: ½ cup*

¼ cup finely chopped pitted green olives
¼ cup finely chopped pitted Kalamata olives
1 tablespoon finely chopped parsley
1 tablespoon extra-virgin olive oil
1 teaspoon fresh lemon zest
1 teaspoon fresh lemon juice
⅛ teaspoon ground black pepper

- In a small bowl, combine green olives, Kalamata olives, parsley, olive oil, lemon zest, lemon juice, and pepper, stirring to blend. Cover, and refrigerate until needed, up to 2 days.

Tomato-Dill Shortbreads with Olive Salad
Yield: 40 to 42

1 cup all-purpose flour
½ cup finely grated Parmesan cheese
¼ cup tomato paste
3 tablespoons finely chopped fresh dill
1 teaspoon granulated sugar
¼ teaspoon salt
¼ teaspoon ground black pepper
5 tablespoons cold, salted butter, cut into pieces
1 recipe Olive Salad (recipe follows)

- In the work bowl of a food processor, combine flour, cheese, tomato paste, dill, sugar, salt, and pepper, pulsing until tomato paste is evenly distributed. Add butter, and pulse until dough comes together.
- Turn out dough onto a sheet of plastic wrap. Using a rolling pin, flatten into a disk. Wrap securely, and refrigerate for 2 hours.
- Preheat oven to 350°.
- Line 2 rimmed baking sheets with parchment paper.
- Turn out dough onto a lightly floured surface. Using a rolling pin, roll out dough to a ¼-inch thickness. Using a 2¼-inch flower-shaped cutter, cut as many shapes as possible from dough. Place shortbreads 2 inches apart on prepared baking sheets.
- Bake until edges are light golden brown, 11 to 13 minutes. Transfer shortbreads to a wire cooling rack, and let cool completely. Store in an airtight container.

White Chocolate Blondies
Yield: 24

½ cup salted butter, softened
1 cup firmly packed light brown sugar
2 large eggs
1 teaspoon vanilla extract
2 cups all-purpose flour
1 tablespoon fresh lime zest
2 teaspoons baking powder
½ teaspoon salt
1 cup (approximately 6 ounces) coarsely chopped white chocolate, such as Ghirardelli
½ cup chopped toasted walnuts
1 (4-ounce) bar white chocolate, such as Ghirardelli

- Preheat oven to 350°.
- Line a 13x9-inch pan with foil, letting edges of foil hang over sides. Lightly spray foil with cooking spray.
- In a large mixing bowl, beat butter at high speed with a mixer until creamy. Add brown sugar, beating until light and fluffy. Add eggs and vanilla extract, beating to combine.
- In a medium bowl, combine flour, lime zest, baking powder, and salt, whisking well. Add flour mixture to butter mixture, beating at medium speed until incorporated. Add chopped white chocolate and walnuts, beating until incorporated. Spread batter into prepared pan, smoothing with a spatula to create a level surface.

- Bake until blondie is light golden brown and a wooden pick inserted in the center comes out clean, approximately 20 minutes. Let cool completely in pan.
- Lift blondie from pan, using excess foil as handles. Place on a cutting board.
- Melt remaining white chocolate bar according to package directions. Transfer melted white chocolate to a piping bag fitted with a small, round tip or to a resealable plastic bag with tip of a corner snipped off. Pipe melted white chocolate in a diagonal pattern across whole block of blondie. Let set until white chocolate is firm.
- Using a long sharp knife, cut blondie into 24 bars, pressing evenly downward.
- Store at room temperature in an airtight container with layers separated by wax paper.

Lemon-Basil Cookies
Yield: 48

⅓ cup salted butter, softened
½ cup confectioners' sugar
½ cup granulated sugar
1 large egg
1 large egg yolk
2 teaspoons lemon extract
¼ teaspoon vanilla extract
1 tablespoon fresh lemon zest
1¾ cups cake flour
3 tablespoons finely chopped fresh basil
½ teaspoon baking powder
¼ teaspoon salt
Garnish: additional confectioners' sugar

- Preheat oven to 325°.
- Line several rimmed baking sheets with parchment paper.
- In a large mixing bowl, beat butter at high speed with a mixer until creamy. Add confectioners' sugar and granulated sugar, beating until light and fluffy. Add egg and egg yolk, beating until incorporated. Add lemon extract, vanilla extract, and lemon zest, beating until incorporated.
- In a medium bowl, combine flour, basil, baking powder, and salt, whisking well. Add flour mixture to butter mixture, beating until incorporated. (Dough will be sticky.) Divide dough into 1-teaspoon portions, and roll gently with floured hands to make balls. Place dough balls 2 inches apart on prepared baking sheets. Dip bottom of a glass into flour, and press down gently on tops of cookies to flatten.
- Bake until edges are very light golden brown, 10 to 11 minutes. Transfer cookies to a wire rack, and let cool completely.

- Just before serving, garnish cookies with a dusting of confectioners' sugar, if desired.
- Store at room temperature in an airtight container with layers separated by wax paper.

MAKE-AHEAD TIP: Lemon-Basil Cookies can be made a week advance, placed in an airtight container, and frozen. Let thaw completely before garnishing with confectioners' sugar.

soda, whisking well. Add flour mixture to butter mixture in thirds, alternately with buttermilk, beginning and ending with flour mixture. Add food coloring until desired shade of pink is achieved. Spoon batter into prepared pan. Tap pan firmly on countertop to level batter and reduce air bubbles.
• Bake until a wooden pick inserted near the center comes out clean, approximately 80 minutes. (Cover cake lightly with foil during baking to prevent excess browning, if necessary.) Let cake cool in pan for 10 minutes.
• Using a long serrated knife, trim dome from cake, if desired, to level top.
• Turn out cake onto a wire cooling rack, and let cool completely.
• Place wire rack over a rimmed baking sheet. Spoon Strawberry Glaze over cake, and let dry completely.
• Just before serving, garnish cake with fresh strawberries, if desired.

We used a Nordic Ware Bavaria Bundt Pan.

MAKE-AHEAD TIP: *Cake can be baked a week in advance, placed in an airtight container, and frozen. Let thaw completely before glazing.*

Strawberry Mini Bundt Cakes
Yield: 24

½ cup unsalted butter, softened
1¼ cups granulated sugar
¼ cup firmly packed light brown sugar
3 teaspoons strawberry extract
3 large eggs, at room temperature
2 cups all-purpose flour
¼ teaspoon salt
⅛ teaspoon baking soda
½ cup whole buttermilk
Pink paste food coloring, such as Wilton
1 recipe Strawberry Glaze (recipe follows)
Garnish: finely chopped strawberries

• Preheat oven to 325°.
• Spray the wells of 2 (12-well) mini Bundt cake pans* with baking spray with flour.
• In a large mixing bowl, beat butter at high speed with a mixer until creamy. Add sugar, brown sugar, and strawberry extract, beating until light and fluffy. Add eggs, one at a time, beating well after each addition.
• In a medium bowl, combine flour, salt, and baking soda, whisking well. Add flour mixture to butter mixture in thirds, alternately with buttermilk, beginning and ending with flour mixture. Add food coloring until desired

Strawberry Bundt Cake
Yield: 16 servings

1 cup unsalted butter, softened
2 cups granulated sugar
½ cup firmly packed light brown sugar
2 tablespoons strawberry extract
4 large eggs, at room temperature
3 cups all-purpose flour
½ teaspoon salt
¼ teaspoon baking soda
1 cup whole buttermilk
Pink paste food coloring, such as Wilton
1 recipe Strawberry Glaze (recipe on page 102)
Garnish: fresh strawberries

• Preheat oven to 325°.
• Spray a 10-cup Bundt cake pan* with baking spray with flour.
• In a large mixing bowl, beat butter at high speed with a mixer until creamy. Add sugar, brown sugar, and strawberry extract, beating until light and fluffy. Add eggs, one at a time, beating well after each addition.
• In a medium bowl, combine flour, salt, and baking

shade of pink is achieved. Divide batter evenly among wells of prepared pans. Tap pans firmly on countertop to level batter and reduce air bubbles.

• Bake until a wooden pick inserted in the centers of cakes comes out clean, 18 to 20 minutes. Let cakes cool in pans for 10 minutes. Remove from pans, and transfer to wire cooling racks. Let cool completely.

• Place each wire rack over a rimmed baking sheet. Spoon Strawberry Glaze over cakes, and let dry completely.

• Store at room temperature in an airtight container.

• Just before serving, fill centers of cakes with chopped strawberries.

• Serve immediately.

We used Wilton Perfect Results 12-well fluted tube cake pans, available at wilton.com.

MAKE-AHEAD TIP: Cakes can be baked a week in advance, placed in an airtight container, and frozen. Let thaw completely before glazing.

Strawberry Glaze

Gluten-free | *Yield: 1½ cups*

4½ cups confectioners' sugar
½ cup plus 1 tablespoon whole milk
2¼ teaspoons strawberry extract*

• In a large bowl, combine confectioners' sugar, milk, and strawberry extract, whisking until smooth and creamy. Use immediately.

*If extract is not pink, tint glaze with food coloring, if desired.

Retirement

The
MENU

SCONE
Sour Cream Scones
Orange Cranberry Black Tea

SAVORIES
Salmon Canapés
with Mustard-Caper Butter

Cucumber-Tarragon
Chicken Salad Sandwiches

Beef and Bruschetta
Crostini

Ceylon Highlands Black Tea

SWEETS
Strawberry-Topped
Vanilla Shortbread

Coconut Cakes with
Lemon–White Chocolate
Buttercream

Chocolate-Hazelnut Tartlets

*Rooibos French Vanilla
Herbal Tea*

*Tea Pairings by Simpson & Vail, Inc.,
800-282-8327, svtea.com*

*Buffets laden with
hot tea and delicious
scones, savories, and
sweets offer superb
ways to recognize
the culmination of a
successful career.*

> *"The afternoon knows what the morning never suspected."*
>
> —ROBERT FROST

Sour Cream Scones
Yield: 20

4 cups all-purpose flour
½ cup granulated sugar
4 teaspoons baking powder
1 teaspoon salt
½ teaspoon baking soda
2 teaspoons lemon zest
8 tablespoons cold unsalted butter, cut into pieces
1 cup sour cream
¾ cup plus 2 tablespoons cold heavy whipping
   cream, divided
¼ teaspoon vanilla extract
¼ teaspoon lemon extract

• Preheat oven to 350°.
• Line 2 rimmed baking sheets with parchment paper.
• In a large bowl, combine flour, sugar, baking powder, salt, baking soda, and lemon zest, whisking well. Using a pastry blender, cut butter into flour mixture until it resembles coarse crumbs.
• In a small bowl, combine sour cream, ¾ cup whipping cream, vanilla extract, and lemon extract, stirring well. Add to flour mixture, stirring until evenly moist. (If dough seems dry, add more whipping cream, 1 tablespoon at a time.) Working gently, bring mixture together with hands until a dough forms.
• Turn out dough onto a lightly floured surface. Knead gently 4 to 5 times. Using a rolling pin, roll dough to a 1-inch thickness. Using a 2-inch fluted round cutter, cut 20 scones from dough. Place scones 2 inches apart on prepared baking sheets.
• Brush tops of scones with remaining 2 tablespoons cream.
• Bake until edges are golden brown and a wooden pick inserted in the centers comes out clean, approximately 20 minutes.
• Serve warm.

RECOMMENDED CONDIMENTS:
Clotted Cream
Raspberry Preserves
Lemon Curd

Salmon Canapés with Mustard-Caper Butter
Yield: 24

6 slices rye bread, frozen
1 (4-ounce) package sliced smoked salmon
2 tablespoons salted butter, at room temperature
1 teaspoon stone-ground Dijon-style mustard
½ teaspoon finely chopped capers
⅛ teaspoon ground black pepper
1 tablespoon extra-virgin olive oil
Garnish: fresh dill sprigs

• Using a 1½-inch round cutter, cut 24 rounds from frozen bread, discarding scraps. Place bread rounds in a resealable plastic bag to thaw.
• Using the same cutter, cut 24 rounds from salmon slices, discarding scraps.
• In a small bowl, combine butter, mustard, capers, and pepper, stirring until well blended.
• Using an offset spatula, spread a layer of butter mixture onto bread rounds. Top butter layer with a salmon round. Brush salmon with olive oil.
• Garnish each canapé with a fresh dill sprig, if desired.
• Serve immediately.

MAKE-AHEAD TIP: Bread rounds can be prepared a day ahead and stored in a resealable plastic bag at room temperature. Salmon rounds can be prepared a day ahead, placed in an airtight container, and refrigerated until needed.

Cucumber-Tarragon Chicken Salad Sandwiches
Yield: 32

¾ cup plus ⅔ cup mayonnaise, divided
3 tablespoons chopped fresh tarragon
1 tablespoon fresh lemon juice
¼ teaspoon salt
¼ teaspoon ground black pepper
4 cups chopped roast chicken*
32 slices firm white sandwich bread, frozen
1 English cucumber
2 cups spring mix lettuce

• In a large bowl, combine ¾ cup mayonnaise, tarragon, lemon juice, salt, and pepper, stirring until well blended. Add chicken, stirring until incorporated.
• Using a 2¾-inch square cutter, cut 32 shapes from frozen bread, discarding scraps. Place in a resealable plastic bag to thaw, or cover with damp paper towels to prevent drying out.
• Using a mandoline or a sharp paring knife, cut 96 very thin slices from cucumber. Blot cucumber slices dry with paper towels.
• Spread a layer of remaining ⅔ cup mayonnaise onto each bread square. Spread approximately ¼ cup chicken salad onto mayonnaise side of 16 bread squares. Top each with 6 cucumber slices, a single layer of lettuce, and another bread slice, mayonnaise side down.
• Using a serrated bread knife, cut sandwiches in half diagonally.
• Serve immediately.

Process roast chicken meat in the work bowl of a food processor to chop finely.

MAKE-AHEAD TIP: Chicken salad can be made a day ahead, covered, and refrigerated.

Beef and Bruschetta Crostini
Yield: 24

2 (6- to 8-ounce) beef filets mignons
2 tablespoons olive oil, divided
¼ teaspoon garlic powder
¼ teaspoon salt
¼ teaspoon coarsely ground black pepper
1 long thin French baguette
1 clove garlic, cut in half
2 tablespoons melted butter
1 recipe Tomato-Basil Bruschetta (recipe follows)

• Preheat oven to 350°.
• Line a rimmed baking sheet with foil.
• Rub filets with 1 tablespoon olive oil, and season with garlic powder, salt, and pepper, rubbing spices into meat.
• In a medium nonstick sauté pan, heat remaining 1 tablespoon olive oil over medium-high heat. When oil shimmers and pan is hot, add filets, searing on all sides until brown. Transfer filets to prepared baking sheet, and place in oven to finish cooking until beef is medium rare, 10 to 15 minutes. (Cook longer until desired degree of doneness is achieved.) Remove from oven, and let rest for 10 minutes.
• Using a long sharp knife, slice filet across the grain into ¼-inch pieces. Wrap slices in foil to keep warm.
• Line a rimmed baking sheet with parchment paper.
• Using a serrated bread knife, slice baguette at an angle into ½-inch pieces. Rub each slice with cut edge of garlic. Place baguette slices on prepared baking sheet. Brush melted butter onto each baguette slice.
• Bake baguette slices until light golden brown, 5 to 7 minutes.
• Place a beef slice on each toasted baguette slice, cutting beef to fit, if necessary. Using a slotted spoon or a fork so liquid drains well, top beef with Tomato-Basil Bruschetta.
• Serve immediately.

MAKE-AHEAD TIP: Beef filets can be prepared a day ahead, wrapped in foil, and refrigerated. Slice and warm just before serving. Tomato-Basil Bruschetta can be prepared a day ahead, covered, and refrigerated until needed.

Tomato-Basil Bruschetta
Gluten-free | Yield: 1 cup

2 tablespoons olive oil, divided
1 tablespoon minced garlic
1 cup finely diced Campari tomatoes
3 tablespoons chopped fresh basil
¼ teaspoon salt
⅛ teaspoon ground black pepper
3 tablespoons red wine vinegar

• In a small nonstick sauté pan, heat 1 tablespoon olive oil over medium-low heat. Add garlic, and cook just until very lightly golden, approximately 1 minute. Remove from heat.
• In a medium bowl, combine garlic, tomatoes, basil, salt, pepper, vinegar, and remaining 1 tablespoon olive oil, tossing until well blended.

wheel, etch lines into dough, running wheel in vertical lines approximately ¼ inch apart. (If a pastry wheel is not available, a fork may be used instead.)
• Bake shortbread until light golden brown, approximately 50 minutes.
• Let cool completely on a wire rack. Using foil overhang as handles, lift shortbread from pan, and place on a cutting surface. Remove foil from bottom of shortbread.
• Using a long sharp knife, cut 32 (2-inch) squares, pressing down to create clean cuts. Store shortbread squares in an airtight container at room temperature for up to a day until ready to serve.
• Garnish shortbread squares with a dusting of confectioners' sugar and with strawberry halves, if desired.

Coconut Cakes with Lemon–White Chocolate Buttercream
Yield: 48 servings

3 cups cake flour, such as Swans Down
1 tablespoon baking powder
½ teaspoon salt
1 cup unsalted butter, softened
2 cups granulated sugar
4 large eggs
2 teaspoons coconut extract
½ teaspoon vanilla extract
1 cup whole milk
1 recipe Lemon–White Chocolate Buttercream
  (recipe follows)
Garnish: toasted sweetened shredded coconut

• Preheat oven to 350°.
• Spray an 18x13-inch rimmed baking sheet with cooking spray. Line with parchment paper, and spray again.
• In a medium bowl, combine cake flour, baking powder, and salt, whisking well.
• In a large mixing bowl, beat butter at medium speed with a mixer until creamy. Gradually add sugar, beating until light and fluffy, approximately 3 minutes. Add eggs, one at a time, beating well after each addition. Add coconut extract and vanilla extract, beating well. Add flour mixture to butter mixture in thirds, alternately with milk, beginning and ending with flour mixture. Pour batter into prepared baking sheet, and spread evenly. Tap baking sheet sharply on countertop to reduce air bubbles.
• Bake until a wooden pick inserted in the center comes out clean, 15 to 16 minutes. Let cool completely in baking sheet on a wire rack.

Strawberry-Topped Vanilla Shortbread
Yield: 32 squares

2 cups unsalted butter, softened
1 cup confectioners' sugar
⅔ cup firmly packed light brown sugar
2 teaspoons vanilla extract
4 cups all-purpose flour
½ teaspoon salt
Garnish: confectioners' sugar and fresh strawberry
  halves

• Preheat oven to 300°.
• Line a 13x9-inch pan with foil, letting foil hang over sides, and spray with cooking spray.
• In a large mixing bowl, combine butter, confectioners' sugar, brown sugar, and vanilla extract. Beat at medium-high speed with a mixer until light and creamy, 2 to 3 minutes.
• In a medium bowl, combine flour and salt, whisking well. Add to butter mixture, beating just until incorporated.
• Press dough into prepared pan. Using a pastry

- Invert cake onto a large wire rack. Remove parchment paper from cake bottom. Invert cake onto a cutting surface, top side up. Using a long sharp knife, trim and discard edges from cake. Spread Lemon–White Chocolate Buttercream in an even layer onto top of cake.
- Just before serving, cut cake into 42 (2½x1½-inch) pieces, wiping knife between cuts.
- Garnish cake pieces with toasted coconut, if desired.

MAKE-AHEAD TIP: Cake can be baked in advance, wrapped tightly in plastic wrap while still in the baking sheet, and frozen for up to a week. Remove from pan, and let come to room temperature before spreading with buttercream.

Lemon–White Chocolate Buttercream
Gluten-free | *Yield: 3½ cups*

6 cups confectioners' sugar
1½ cups unsalted butter, at room temperature
½ teaspoon salt
3 tablespoons fresh lemon juice
2 (4-ounce) Baker's Premium White Chocolate Baking Chocolate Bars, melted and cooled

- In a large mixing bowl, combine confectioners' sugar, butter, salt, and lemon juice. Beat at medium speed with a mixer, gradually increasing speed to high, until smooth and creamy. Add melted white chocolate, beating until incorporated.
- Use immediately, or transfer to an airtight container, and refrigerate until needed, up to a day. (Before using buttercream, let soften slightly at room temperature; beat with a mixer for 1 minute.)

2½-inch round cutter, cut 22 rounds from pie dough. Press dough into prepared tartlet pans, discarding excess dough. Using a chopstick, push pie dough into indentations in sides of tartlet pans. Place prepared tartlet pans on a rimmed baking sheet. Refrigerate for 30 minutes, or freeze for 15 minutes.
• Prick bottoms of pie dough with a fork to prevent puffing during baking.
• Bake until very light golden brown, 5 to 7 minutes. Let cool completely on baking sheet.
• Reduce oven temperature to 350°.
• In a medium bowl, combine egg, brown sugar, corn syrup, melted butter, and vanilla extract, whisking well. Add hazelnuts, stirring to combine. Divide mixture among prepared tartlet shells, filling three-fourths full.
• Bake until filling is set and puffed, 13 to 15 minutes. Let cool completely in pans.
• Carefully remove tartlets from pans onto a rimmed baking sheet.
• Spread warm Chocolate Ganache onto tartlets.
• Garnish tartlets with a sprinkle of additional chopped hazelnuts, if desired.
• Refrigerate until chocolate is firm, approximately 1 hour and up to a day.
• Just before serving, place Sweetened Whipped Cream in a piping bag fitted with a large open-star tip (Wilton #1M), and pipe a rosette of cream onto each tartlet.

Chocolate Ganache
Gluten-free | *Yield: ⅓ cup*

3 tablespoons heavy whipping cream
1 (4-ounce) bar semisweet chocolate, such as
    Ghirardelli, finely chopped

• In a small saucepan, heat cream over medium-high heat until very hot. Remove from heat, and add chocolate, stirring until chocolate melts and mixture is smooth.
• Use immediately.

Sweetened Whipped Cream
Gluten-free | *Yield: 2 cups*

1 cup cold heavy whipping cream
3 tablespoons confectioners' sugar
¼ teaspoon vanilla extract

• In a large mixing bowl, combine cream, confectioners' sugar, and vanilla extract. Beat at high speed with a mixer until stiff peaks form. Cover and refrigerate until needed.

Chocolate-Hazelnut Tartlets
Yield: 22

1 (14.1-ounce) package refrigerated pie dough
    (2 sheets)
1 large egg
½ cup firmly packed light brown sugar
3 tablespoons light corn syrup
1 tablespoon salted butter, melted
½ teaspoon vanilla extract
½ cup plus 2 tablespoons finely chopped roasted
    hazelnuts
1 recipe Chocolate Ganache (recipe follows)
1 recipe Sweetened Whipped Cream (recipe follows)
Garnish: additional chopped roasted hazelnuts

• Preheat oven to 450°.
• Lightly spray 22 (2¼-inch) round tartlet pans with cooking spray. Place on a rimmed baking sheet.
• Unroll pie dough on a lightly floured surface. Using a rolling pin, roll each sheet slightly larger. Using a

Tartlet Crust
How-Tos
ON PAGE 130

Golden
ANNIVERSARY

The
MENU

SCONE
Apricot-Orange Scones
Milk Oolong

SAVORIES
Shrimp Salad Canapés
Roast Beef and Cucumber
Finger Sandwiches
Chicken Cordon Bleu Spirals
Organic Capital Breakfast

SWEETS
Golden Heart Cookies
Maple-Pecan Tartlets
Lemon-Vanilla
Anniversary Cakes
Madame Butterfly Jasmine

Tea Pairings by Capital Teas,
888-484-8327, capitalteas.com

*A 50th wedding
anniversary calls
for an elegant and
romantic ambiance to
celebrate a couple that
exemplify a life of love
and happiness.*

Place scones 2 inches apart on prepared baking sheet.
• Brush tops of scones with remaining 1 tablespoon cream.
• Bake until edges of scones are golden brown and a wooden pick inserted in the centers comes out clean, approximately 20 minutes.
• Serve warm.

RECOMMENDED CONDIMENTS:
Clotted Cream
Orange Marmalade

Shrimp Salad Canapés
Yield: 15

12 ounces peeled and deveined cooked shrimp
¼ cup mayonnaise
1½ tablespoons cocktail sauce
1 teaspoon fresh lemon zest
¼ teaspoon salt
¼ teaspoon hot pepper sauce, such as Tabasco
⅛ teaspoon ground black pepper
1 tablespoon chopped green onion tops
1 (1.9-ounce) box mini phyllo cups, such as Athens

• In the work bowl of a food processor, pulse shrimp until finely chopped.
• In a medium bowl, combine mayonnaise, cocktail sauce, lemon zest, salt, hot pepper sauce, and black pepper, stirring well. Add shrimp and green onion, stirring until incorporated.
• Cover and refrigerate until cold, approximately 4 hours.
• Just before serving, divide shrimp salad among phyllo cups.

Apricot-Orange Scones
Yield: 12

2 cups all-purpose flour
⅓ cup granulated sugar
2 teaspoons baking powder
2 teaspoons fresh orange zest
½ teaspoon salt
4 tablespoons cold, unsalted butter
½ cup chopped dried apricots
¾ cup plus 2 tablespoons cold heavy whipping cream, divided
½ teaspoon vanilla extract

• Preheat oven to 350°.
• Line a rimmed baking sheet with parchment paper.
• In a large bowl, combine flour, sugar, baking powder, orange zest, and salt, whisking well. Using a pastry blender, cut butter into flour mixture until it resembles coarse crumbs. Add apricots, stirring until incorporated.
• In a small bowl, combine ¾ cup plus 1 tablespoon cream and vanilla extract, stirring well. Add cream to flour mixture, stirring until mixture is evenly moist. (If dough seems dry, add more cream, 1 tablespoon at a time.) Working gently, bring mixture together with hands until a dough forms.
• Turn out dough onto a lightly floured surface. Knead lightly 4 to 5 times. Using a rolling pin, roll dough to a ¾-inch thickness. Using a 2¼-inch fluted round cutter, cut 12 scones from dough, rerolling scraps as necessary.

Roast Beef and Cucumber Finger Sandwiches
Yield: 12

8 slices firm white sandwich bread
4 large thin slices deli roast beef
1 English cucumber
½ cup watercress
1 recipe Horseradish Aïoli (recipe follows)
Garnish: additional watercress

• Using a serrated bread knife, trim and discard crusts from bread slices. Cut each bread square evenly into 3 rectangles (fingers). To prevent drying out, place bread rectangles in a resealable plastic bag or cover with damp paper towels.

- Cut 12 slices from roast beef, making each one-third longer than length of bread rectangles and double the width.
- Using a mandoline or a sharp knife, cut 36 very thin slices from cucumber.
- Spread aïoli in an even layer onto bread rectangles. Fold roast beef slices in half lengthwise, and gather each to fit onto aïoli side of 12 bread rectangles. Shingle 3 cucumber slices atop each, and top with watercress and remaining bread rectangles, aïoli side down.
- Garnish with additional watercress, if desired.

Horseradish Aïoli
Gluten-free | *Yield: ¼ cup*

¼ cup mayonnaise
2 teaspoons fresh ground horseradish
⅛ teaspoon salt
⅛ teaspoon ground black pepper

- In a small bowl, combine mayonnaise, horseradish, salt, and pepper, stirring until blended.
- Use immediately.

Chicken Cordon Bleu Spirals
Yield: 12

½ (17.5-ounce) package frozen puff pastry
  (1 sheet)
2 tablespoons stone-ground Dijon mustard
4 large thin slices deli Black Forest ham
4 large thin slices deli roast chicken
½ cup grated Gruyère cheese
½ teaspoon fresh thyme leaves
½ teaspoon fresh chopped chives
⅛ teaspoon ground black pepper
1 large egg
1 tablespoon water
Garnish: fresh snipped chives

- Preheat oven to 400°.
- Line a rimmed baking sheet with parchment paper.
- Let puff pastry thaw just enough to be able to roll up and encase filling. (It should still be cold and firm.)
- Unroll puff pastry sheet on a lightly floured surface. Using a rolling pin, roll out puff pastry until smooth. Spread mustard over puff pastry evenly. Arrange ham slices over mustard. Top with chicken slices. Scatter cheese over chicken slices. Sprinkle thyme, chives, and pepper over cheese. Starting at a long end, roll up pastry firmly and evenly to encase ingredients and form a cylinder. Tuck ends under.
- Using a serrated knife in a sawing motion, cut

12 slices. Place slices 2 inches apart on remaining prepared baking sheet.
- In a small bowl, combine egg and water, whisking to blend. Brush slices with egg mixture.
- Bake until golden brown, approximately 15 minutes.
- Garnish with snipped chives, if desired.
- Serve immediately.

MAKE-AHEAD TIP: Puff pastry can be assembled a day in advance, and cylinder can be wrapped in plastic wrap and refrigerated. Just before serving, unwrap, slice, brush with egg mixture, and bake.

- In a large mixing bowl, combine butter and sugar. Beat at high speed with a mixer until light and fluffy, approximately 5 minutes. Add egg and vanilla extract, beating until incorporated. Gradually add flour mixture to butter mixture, beating until dough comes together.
- Divide dough in half. Place one portion of dough between 2 sheets of wax paper. Using a rolling pin, roll dough to a ⅛-inch thickness. Transfer dough and wax paper to a rimmed baking sheet, and freeze for 15 minutes. Repeat with remaining dough.
- Remove wax paper. Using a 2-inch heart-shaped cutter, cut 96 shapes from chilled dough. Place cookies 2 inches apart on prepared baking sheets.
- Bake until edges are very light golden brown, 9 to 10 minutes. Transfer cookies to wire racks. Let cool completely.
- Store cookies in airtight containers with layers separated by wax paper until ready to serve.
- Just before serving, pipe dulce de leche onto bottom side of 48 cookies, following outline of heart and filling in. Top each with remaining cookies, flat sides together.
- If desired, using a small pastry paintbrush, lightly coat tops of cookies with gold pearl dust powder.

Maple-Pecan Tartlets
Yield: 20

1 (14.1-ounce) package refrigerated pie dough (2 sheets)
1 large egg
¼ cup firmly packed light brown sugar
2 tablespoons maple syrup
1 tablespoon melted butter
½ teaspoon vanilla extract
⅛ teaspoon salt
¾ cup finely chopped toasted pecans
1 recipe Sweetened Whipped Cream (recipe follows)
Garnish: additional finely chopped toasted pecans

- Preheat oven to 450°.
- Lightly spray 20 (2¼-inch) round tartlet pans with cooking spray.
- Unroll pie dough on a lightly floured surface. Using a 2½-inch round cutter, cut 20 rounds from pie dough. Press dough into prepared tartlet pans, discarding excess dough. Using a chopstick, push pie dough into indentations in sides of tartlet pans. Place prepared tartlet pans on a rimmed baking sheet. Freeze for 15 minutes.
- Prick bottoms of pie dough with a fork to prevent puffing during baking.

Golden Heart Cookies
Yield: 48

3 cups all-purpose flour
1½ teaspoons baking powder
¾ teaspoon salt
1 cup unsalted butter, softened
1 cup granulated sugar
1 large egg
½ teaspoon vanilla extract
1 (13.4-ounce) can dulce de leche, such as Nestlé
Garnish: gold pearl dust powder, such as Wilton

- Preheat oven to 350°.
- Line several rimmed baking sheets with parchment paper.
- In medium bowl, combine flour, baking powder, and salt, whisking well.

- Bake until light golden brown, 5 to 7 minutes. Let cool completely.
- In a medium bowl, combine egg, brown sugar, maple syrup, melted butter, vanilla extract, and salt, stirring well. Add pecans, stirring until incorporated. Divide mixture evenly among prepared tartlet shells.
- Bake until filling is set, 12 to 13 minutes. Let cool slightly before carefully removing from pans. Let cool completely on a wire rack.
- Just before serving, place Sweetened Whipped Cream in a piping bag fitted with a large open-star tip (Wilton #1M). Pipe a rosette of whipped cream onto each tartlet.
- Garnish tartlets with additional finely chopped toasted pecans, if desired.

MAKE-AHEAD TIP: Tartlets can be made a day ahead, placed in an airtight container, and refrigerated until needed. Pipe whipped cream, and garnish just before serving.

Sweetened Whipped Cream
Gluten-free | *Yield: 1 cup*

½ cup cold heavy whipping cream
1 tablespoon confectioners' sugar
¼ teaspoon vanilla extract

- In a small mixing bowl, combine cream, confectioners' sugar, and vanilla extract. Beat at high speed with a mixer until stiff peaks form. Cover, and refrigerate until needed, up to 3 hours.

Tartlet Crust
How-Tos
ON PAGE 130

Lemon-Vanilla Anniversary Cakes
Yield: 24

¾ cup unsalted butter, softened, divided
1¾ cups plus 3 tablespoons cake flour,
    such as Swans Down, divided
½ cup plus 3 tablespoons granulated sugar
1 large egg
1 tablespoon fresh lemon zest
1½ teaspoons baking powder
¼ teaspoon salt
½ cup whole milk
½ teaspoon lemon extract
½ teaspoon vanilla extract
2 recipes Vanilla Glaze (recipe follows)
1 recipe Vanilla Buttercream (recipe follows)
1 (5.8-ounce) package scroll-patterned fondant
    ribbon, such as Wilton*
24 (4mm) gold dragées, such as N.Y. Cake

• Preheat oven to 350°.
• Using fingers, coat the wells of a 24-well 2-tier cake pop pan† evenly with ¼ cup butter. Sift ¼ cup cake flour over prepared wells of pan. Tilt and shake pan to ensure flour coats wells evenly. Turn pan over, and tap out and discard excess flour.
• In a large mixing bowl, combine remaining ½ cup butter and sugar. Beat at high speed with a mixer until light and fluffy, approximately 3 minutes. Add egg and lemon zest, beating until incorporated.
• In a medium bowl, combine remaining 1½ cups plus 3 tablespoons cake flour, baking powder, and salt, whisking well.
• In a small bowl, combine milk, lemon extract, and vanilla extract, stirring well. With mixer running at low speed, add flour mixture to butter mixture in thirds, alternately with milk mixture, beginning and ending with flour mixture and beating just until incorporated. Using a 1½-tablespoon levered scoop, drop batter into wells of prepared pan. Tap pan to level batter.
• Bake until edges are golden brown and a wooden pick inserted in the centers comes out clean, approximately 14 minutes. Let cakes cool in pan for 10 minutes.
• Using a serrated knife, cut domes off cakes so cakes will sit level when removed from pan. Turn out cakes onto a wire cooling rack. Let cool completely.
• Place cakes in a single layer in airtight containers, and let sit overnight at room temperature.
• Dip cakes in 1 recipe Vanilla Glaze, coating completely. Let glaze drip off as much as possible. Transfer cakes to wax paper, and let dry completely. Trim hardened pooled frosting from bottom of cakes. Repeat process with remaining 1 recipe Vanilla Glaze.

• Cut 24 lengths of fondant ribbon to fit around cake bases. Wrap a fondant ribbon length around base of each cake, pressing together with fingers to secure.
• Place Vanilla Buttercream in a piping bag fitted with a very small round tip (Wilton #4). Pipe a bead border of buttercream around middles of cakes. Using a medium open-star tip (Wilton #21), pipe a buttercream rosette on tops of cakes.
• Garnish each with a gold dragée, if desired.
• Serve immediately, or place in a single layer in airtight containers, and refrigerate until needed, up to a day.

*Wilton Scroll Fondant Ribbon is available from Jo-Ann, joann.com.

†We used a Cake Boss Specialty Nonstick Bakeware 24-Cup Round 2-Tier Cake Pop Pan from Carlo's Bakery, carlosbakery.com. We recommend not using cooking spray for the cake pop pan.

Vanilla Glaze
Gluten-free | Yield: 3 cups

3 cups granulated sugar
1½ cups hot water
¼ teaspoon cream of tartar
2 cups sifted confectioners' sugar
1 teaspoon vanilla extract

• In a medium saucepan, combine granulated sugar, water, and cream of tartar. Bring to a boil over medium-high heat, whisking occasionally until sugar dissolves. Cook until mixture registers 226° on a candy thermometer and looks thin and syrupy. Remove from heat, and let cool to exactly 110°.
• Add confectioners' sugar and vanilla extract, whisking until mixture is smooth. (If glaze seems thin, add more confectioners' sugar, 1 tablespoon at a time, to reach desired consistency.)
• Use immediately.

Vanilla Buttercream
Gluten-free | Yield: 1 cup

2 cups confectioners' sugar
½ cup unsalted butter, softened
1 tablespoon plus 1 teaspoon whole milk
¼ teaspoon salt

• In a medium mixing bowl, combine confectioners' sugar, butter, milk, and salt. Beat at high speed with a mixer until light and fluffy.
• Use immediately.

TEA-STEEPING *Guide*

The quality of the tea served at afternoon tea is as important as the food and the décor. To be sure your infusion is successful every time, here are some basic guidelines to follow.

WATER

Always use the best water possible. If the water tastes good, so will your tea. Heat the water on the stove top or in an electric kettle to the desired temperature. A microwave oven is not recommended.

TEMPERATURE

Heating the water to the correct temperature is arguably one of the most important factors in making a great pot of tea. Pouring boiling water on green, white, or oolong tea leaves can result in a very unpleasant brew. Always refer to the tea purveyor's packaging for specific instructions, but in general, use 170° to 195° water for these delicate tea types. Reserve boiling (212°) water for black and puerh teas, as well as herbal and fruit tisanes.

TEAPOT

If the teapot you plan to use is delicate, warm it with hot tap water first to avert possible cracking. Discard this water before adding the tea leaves or tea bags.

TEA

Use the highest-quality tea you can afford, whether loose leaf or prepackaged in bags or sachets. Remember that these better teas can often be steeped more than once. When using loose-leaf tea, generally use 1 generous teaspoon of dry leaf per 8 ounces of water, and use an infuser basket. For a stronger infusion, add another teaspoonful or two of dry tea leaf.

TIME

As soon as the water reaches the correct temperature for the type of tea, pour it over the leaves or tea bag in the teapot, and cover the pot with a lid. Set a timer—usually 1 to 2 minutes for whites and oolongs; 2 to 3 minutes for greens; and 3 to 5 minutes for blacks, puerhs, and herbals. (Steeping tea longer than recommended can yield a bitter infusion.) When the timer goes off, remove the infuser basket or the tea bags from the teapot.

ENJOYMENT

For best flavor, serve the tea as soon as possible. Keep the beverage warm atop a lighted warmer or under your favorite tea cozy if necessary.

Cucumber Flower
Canapés
PAGE 75

How-to

Let these step-by-step photos serve as your visual guide while you create these impressive and delicious teatime treats.

CUCUMBER FLOWER

1

Fold each cucumber slice in half and then in quarters.

2

Pinch the inner fold between your thumb and forefinger.

3

Place on a bread square, green edges up. Repeat 3 times.

4

Arrange folds to resemble a flower, and top with lemon zest.

Chocolate-Hazelnut
Tartlets
PAGE 113

TARTLET CRUST

1

Using a cutter, cut shapes from dough.

2

Press dough shapes into tartlet pans.

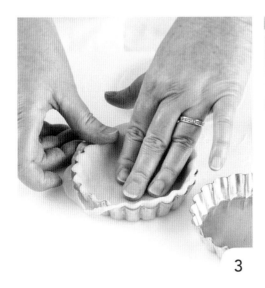

3

Trim excess dough.

4

Using the wide end of a chopstick, push dough into indentations of pan.

Chicken
Cordon Bleu Spirals
PAGE 120

Acknowledgments

COVER
Photography by William Dickey
Recipe Development and Food Styling by
Janet Lambert
Royal Winton Old Cottage Chintz Ascot cup and
saucer, bread and butter plate, teapot, and open
sugar bowl; Gorham Strasbourg flatware set;
Jeannette Glass Cherry Blossom pink tumbler*.
Anna's Palette by Anna Weatherley Indigo Blue
charger from DeVine Corp, 732-751-0500,
devinecorp.net. Classic linen table runner†. White
scalloped cake stand from Pier 1, 800-245-4595,
pier1.com. Flower arrangement‡.

BABY GENDER REVEAL
Photography by Jim Bathie
Food Styling by Susan D. Green; Recipe Development
by Susan D. Green and Janet Lambert
Pages 17–28: Wedgwood Gilded Weave 5-piece
place setting, teapot, creamer, and sugar bowl with
lid; Towle King Richard sterling flatware set*. Julia
Knight Peony in Snow 16-inch 3-tiered server,
11.5-inch 2-tiered server, 15-inch hors d'oeuvres
tray from Julia Knight Collection, 800-388-1878,
juliaknightcollection.com. Starburst napkin ring
from Z Gallerie, 800-908-6748, zgallerie.com.
Flower arrangement and vases‡.
Page 22: Tempo square glass tasting bowl**.

CHRISTENING
Photography by William Dickey
Recipe Development and Food Styling by
Kellie Gerber Kelley
Pages 29–38: Lenox Southern Vista 5-piece place
setting, teapot, creamer, 16-inch oval serving
platter, and 2-tiered serving tray*. Mikasa Cameo
Gold flatware set from Mikasa, 866-645-2721,
mikasa.com. Victorian Rose rectangle tablecloth,
Canterbury Classic napkin set from Heritage
Lace, 641-628-4949, heritagelace.com. Crystal
candlesticks from HomeGoods, 800-888-0776,
homegoods.com. Flower arrangements and vases‡.
Page 33: Antique glass egg tray from
Hoover Antique Gallery, 205-822-9500,
hooverantiquegallery.com.

FIRST TEA PARTY
Photography by Jim Bathie
Recipe Development and Food Styling by
Elizabeth Stringer
Pages 39–48: Two-tiered server, china, flowers,
place mats, and pink scone tray courtesy of
CeCe Designs and Events LLC, 205-317-1413,
cecedesignsllc.com. Wallace Queens 65-piece
flatware set from Mikasa, 866-645-2721,
mikasa.com. Teapot**. Wrap Around Tea Cozy
English Rose Pink, Wrap Around Tea Cozy Pink
Parlor from Thistledown Cozies, 877-890-9106,
thistledowncozies.com. Lace-trim pink chambray
napkins from Pier 1, 800-245-4595, pier1.com.
Page 48: Three-tiered server from Maryland China
Company, 800-638-3880, marylandchina.com.

SWEET SIXTEEN
Photography by Marcy Black Simpson
Recipe Development and Food Styling by
Janet Lambert
Pages 49–60: Wedgwood Jasper Conran Floral
5-piece place setting, cream and sugar set, and
teapot from Wedgwood, 877-720-3486,

wedgwood.com. Glass cloche stands, Belgian flax
linen frame napkins, Kenaf table runner, and
hemstitch linen runner†. Cambridge Silversmiths
Emmeline Mirror 51-piece flatware set, Libbey Claret
footed iced tea glasses from Walmart, 800-925-
6278, walmart.com. Floral arrangements and vases‡.
Page 54: Emile Henry ruffled rectangular
platter from Emile Henry USA, 302-326-4800,
emilehenryusa.com.
Page 55: White rimmed rectangular platter**.
Page 60: Jade-colored glass pedestal**.

GRADUATION
Photography by William Dickey
Food Styling by Janet Lambert; Recipe Development
by Virginia Hornbuckle
Pages 61–70: Mottahedeh Chinoise Blue 5-piece
place setting, oval platter, teapot, sugar, and
creamer from Mottahedeh, 800-242-3050,
mottahedeh.com. Gold chargers from Michael's,
800-642-4235, michaels.com. Pottery Barn White
linen hemstitch table runner and Sailor Blue
hemstitch napkin†. Gold flatware from West Elm,
888-922-4119, westelm.com. Floral arrangements
and vases‡.
Page 64: Annieglass Edgey party tray in Gold from
Annieglass, 800-347-6133, annieglass.com.
Page 68: Pearled service tray by Mariposa, 800-
788-1304, mariposa.com.
Page 70: Ivory Saffian Guest Book from Paper
Source, 888-727-3711, papersource.com

ENGAGEMENT
Photography by John O'Hagan
Recipe Development and Food Styling by
Janet Lambert
Pages 71–82: Royal Albert Val d'Or teapot; Towle
King Richard dinner fork, salad fork, teaspoon, and
knife; Fostoria Meadow Rose Blue water goblet*.
Gracie & Co monogrammed notecards from Jane
Lazenby, 205-616-9156, gracieandco.com. Pickard
Signature Collection monogrammed 5-piece place
setting from Pickard, 847-395-3800, pickardchina.
com. Monogrammed ice blue damask napkin from
Bobbins Design, 251-402-3306, bobbinsdesign.com.
Bella Notte Ruffle Edge tablecloth from Bromberg
& Co., 205-871-3276, brombergs.com. Gold lacquer
charger and hammered gold finish napkin ring
from Pier 1, 800-245-4595, pier1.com.
Page 76: Annieglass Ruffle tray from Annieglass,
888-761-0050, annieglass.com.
Page 78: Juliska small pitcher from Juliska, 888-
414-8448, juliska.com.
Page 80: Annieglass Roman Antique tray from
Annieglass, 888-761-0050, annieglass.com.

BRIDAL SHOWER
Photography by William Dickey
Recipe Development and Food Styling by
Janet Lambert
Pages 83–92: Bella Notte quilted place mat in
Amethyst and linen napkin in Amethyst from
Bromberg & Co., 205-871-3276, brombergs.com.
Royal Crown Derby Royal Antoinette dinner plate,
salad plate, bread and butter plate, teapot, cup
and saucer, and serving platter*. Vietri Optical
Drinkware Amethyst water glass from Vietri, 919-
245-4180, vietri.com. Ashland mercury glass votive
from Michaels, 800-799-5176, michaels.com. Floral
arrangements and vases‡.

Page 86: Annieglass Ruffle dinner plate from
Bromberg & Co., 205-871-3276, brombergs.com.
Page 88: Annieglass Roman Antique Gold appetizer
tray from Bromberg & Co., 205-871-3276,
brombergs.com.

BIRTHDAY
Photography by Kamin H. Williams
Recipe Development and Food Styling by
Janet Lambert
Pages 93–102: Royal Winton Old Cottage Chintz
Ascot cup and saucer, dinner plate, bread and
butter plate, teapot, 14-inch oval serving platter,
creamer, and open sugar bowl; Jeannette Glass
Cherry Blossom pink tumbler*. Anna's Palette
by Anna Weatherley Indigo Blue charger and
dessert plate from DeVine Corp, 732-751-0500,
devinecorp.net. Classic linen table runner†. Square
rattan chargers**. Pink berry wreath‡.
Page 101: White scalloped cake stand from Pier 1,
800-245-4595, pier1.com.

RETIREMENT
Photography by John O'Hagan
Recipe Development and Food Styling by
Janet Lambert
Pages 103–114: Silverplate tipping teapot from
Tea for Two, 888-601-9990, teafortwo.com. Royal
Worcester Engagement teapot with lid, footed
cup and saucer, and salad plates; Wedgwood
Sterling teapot with lid, globe-shape creamer,
and globe-shape sugar bowl with lid; Gorham
Chantilly large silverplate waiter tray*. Wallace
Queens 65-piece flatware set from Mikasa, 866-
645-2721, mikasa.com. Mother-of-Pearl utensil
caddy from Pier 1, 800-245-4595, pier1.com.
Flower arrangements and vases‡.
Page 114: International Silver Prelude-Chased
large waiter tray*. Sandwich tongs from Tea for
Two, 888-601-9990, teafortwo.com.

GOLDEN ANNIVERSARY
Photography by Stephanie Welbourne
Recipe Development and Food Styling by
Janet Lambert
Pages 115–123: Haviland Ranson Gold bread
and butter plate; Royal Crown Derby Gold
Aves salad plate; Haviland Dynasty Gold dinner
plate; Arte Italica Vetro-Gold service plate and
goblet; Spode Stafford White flat cup and saucer
set, teapot, creamer, and sugar; Towle Old
Master sterling flatware set*. Carson glass pillar
holders†.
Page 119: Haviland Ranson Gold 10-inch oval
serving platter*.
Page 131: Haviland Ranson Gold 11-inch oval
serving platter*.

* From Replacements, Ltd., 800-REPLACE,
replacements.com
† From Pottery Barn, 888-779-5176,
potterybarn.com
‡ From Flowerbuds Inc., 205-970-3223,
flowerbudsinc.com
** From World Market, 877-967-5362,
worldmarket.com

EDITOR'S NOTE: Items not listed are from private
collections, and no pattern or manufacturer
information is available.

*Mini Strawberry
Flower Tartlets*
PAGE 59

Recipe Index

EDITOR'S NOTE: Recipes listed in blue *are gluten-free, provided gluten-free versions of processed ingredients (such as condiments, precooked meat, stocks, and wraps) are used.*

"Let us be grateful to people who make us happy, they are the charming gardeners who make our souls blossom."

—MARCEL PROUST